Relationship Co-Coaching
A New Approach to
Deeper Love, Less Conflict

Challenging Society's Beliefs About Romance and Marriage

by

Timothy J. McCarthy, PhD

Relationship Co-Coaching: A New Approach to Deeper Love, Less Conflict

All rights reserved. No part of this book may be reproduced, transmitted, downloaded, decompiled, stored in any retrieval system, or translated in any form, or by any means, whether electronic or mechanical without permission in writing from the author.

Copyright © 2015 Timothy J. McCarthy, PhD
Revised, Retitled Edition for E-Book and Paperback
Telemachus Press, LLC
http://www.telemachuspress.com

Copyright © 2011 Timothy J. McCarthy, PhD
First E-Book Publication Under Title of *Co-Coach Yourselves To A Fabulous Relationship*
Published by Telemachus Press

Cover Design by Bryn Bundlie

Visit the author website:
http://www.relationshipcocoaching.com

Softly Specific Co-Coaching[SM] is a service mark of Timothy J. McCarthy, PhD

ISBN: 978-1-937698-58-4 (eBook)
ISBN: 978-1-942899-02-0 (Paperback)

Version 2017.03.29

Praise for *Relationship Co-Coaching*

"Reading this book is like having a conversation with a compassionate, wise, and innovative therapist. Tim McCarthy believes we have the capacity to heal our marriages if we turn towards each other in a new way. The book will enlighten you, challenge you, and show you how to renew your love and reduce your conflict."

—**William J. Doherty**, PhD, professor at the University of Minnesota and author of *Take Back Your Marriage: Sticking Together in a World That Pulls Us Apart*.

"The new book by Dr. Tim McCarthy—*Relationship Co-Coaching: A New Approach to Deeper Love, Less Conflict*—offers valuable guidelines to help couples achieve more closeness, connectedness, and fulfilling relationships. Dr. McCarthy adroitly describes his *relationship co-coaching model*, which focuses on teaching relationship skills (e.g., communication, conflict-management), challenging destructive social messages and beliefs about romantic relationships, and changing ingrained negative patterns. Useful concepts and practical exercises help couples learn to fulfill one another's emotional needs, reduce conflict, communicate respectfully, and achieve unselfish love. This clearly written and insightful book will be extremely helpful for couples striving for greater trust, closeness, and love, and for marital therapists interested in learning effective ways of helping their clients."

—**Terry M. Levy**, PhD, Licensed Clinical Psychologist, Co-director Evergreen Psychotherapy Center, Evergreen, Colorado

"Dr. Tim McCarthy really gets it right when he identifies the need to *challenge society's beliefs about romance and marriage* and proceeds to lay out the important ingredients to developing a rewarding relationship. The idea of *co-coaching* is particularly important because a good marriage is best achieved when partners help each other. Drawing on the best in relational research and a wealth of personal and professional experience Dr. McCarthy lays out an excellent model for couples to use in strengthening their relationships. I have to wonder how much lower the divorce rate would be if every couple used the tools in this book."

—**Kurt Wical,** PhD, LMFT, MN Couple Therapy Center, Roseville, MN

"As psychotherapists we know how absolutely crucial it is to feel loved. Dr. McCarthy addresses this deep human need by offering loving, safe strategies for couples to take ownership for in their relationships. Couples are shown how to identify their negative patterns, learn what their deepest love needs are, and dissipate conflict through highly effective respectful methods. He shows couples how to become their own coaches and control the destiny of their relationship. In particular, his emphasis upon altruistic, unselfish love offers a unique and important perspective not often found in marriage therapy. The exercises are easy for the reader to understand and apply in their own lives. I find the book a great treasure for couples and have used many of the strategies in my own work with clients."

—**Donae Gustafson,** PSY.D, Licensed Clinical Psychologist, Licensed Marriage & Family Therapist, Stillwater, MN

To Barbara, my fantastic wife and best friend
You mean everything to me
And
To all couples working to make their marriages the best they can be

Acknowledgments

First, I want to give appreciation to the many couples that I've worked with who have opened their hearts and shared their personal struggles. Thank you for your trust and willingness to work so hard on your relationships in applying the principles of relationship co-coaching.

I've been fortunate in having received a great deal of help in the development of this book from a number of people. My deepest gratitude goes to my wife who provided tireless copyediting during all phases of the book's development and for the final proofing. In addition, special thanks goes to my son Madigan who took time away from his doctoral studies in English literature at the University of Virginia to give feedback regarding the first draft. Much appreciation is also given to Jocelyn Stone for her excellent assistance in book development, and to graphic designer Bryn Bundlie who created the exceptional cover. I'm grateful to friends and others reviewing the book that provided very important feedback.

Lastly, special recognition is given to the psychologist/marriage therapists who were kind enough to spend time reviewing my book and offering feedback:

Bill Doherty, PhD; Donae Gustafson, PsyD; Karen Hasse, PhD; Terry Levy, PhD; and Kurt Wical, PhD.

To everyone noted, I offer my deepest gratitude and appreciation for taking time from your busy schedules to review the book and make suggestions. Thank you so much!

Contents

Introduction   i
Relationship Co-Coaching: A New Approach To Deeper Love, Less Conflict

Section 1:   1
Co-Coaching for Dynamic Growth

Chapter 1:   3
Challenging Prevailing Beliefs About Romantic Love and Marriage

Chapter 2:   16
Relationship Problems Caused By Failure to Fulfill Unique Love Needs

Chapter 3:   32
The Inevitable Collision of Negative Relationship Patterns (NRPs)

Chapter 4:   46
Co-Coach Yourselves—Break the Cycle of NRPs and Deepen Love!

Chapter 5:   64
Receive Co-Coaching Feedback—Stop Repeating Conflict

Chapter 6:   83
A New Concept of Love for the 21st Century: Altruistic Love and Relationship Self-Actualization

Section 2:   101
Common Relationship Barriers and Sabotage

Chapter 7:   103
Three Sabotaging Beliefs Leading to Premature Break-Up

Chapter 8: 112
The Affair and Its Complications—How to Avoid It!

Chapter 9: 120
Managing Stress in Relationships

Section 3: 129
Love Deepening Skills for Closeness, Affection, and Romance

Chapter 10: 131
Building in the Four Types of Relationship Closeness

Chapter 11: 141
Positives, Love Affirmations, and Romantic Flirting

Chapter 12: 154
Co-Create the Deepest, Most Long-Lasting Love!

Appendix A 158

Appendix B 160

Appendix C 164

Index 166

Notes 172

Relationship Co-Coaching
A New Approach to
Deeper Love, Less Conflict

Challenging Society's Beliefs About Romance and Marriage

Introduction:

Relationship Co-Coaching: A New Approach To Deeper Love, Less Conflict

Society's lack of skills training and commonly accepted cultural beliefs set couples up to have problems and prematurely dissolve their relationships.

It's a struggle to achieve happiness in love and marriage with so many difficulties to overcome. And while it isn't easy, there is no greater achievement in life than a truly successful love relationship.

I'm pleased you've selected this book to consider new ideas for how to improve your relationship. It will give new insights and tools to help you achieve the highest possible happiness in your relationship. A different perspective is offered here regarding relationships, one that is meant to challenge your thinking. If it succeeds, the book may change some of the core beliefs you have accepted, either consciously or subconsciously about romantic relationships, love, and marriage.

No matter what your motivation is for opening this book, no matter where your relationship is right now, there is great opportunity to deepen your love and happiness.

A New Approach to Relationship Success

I'd like to share with you a different approach to relationships. In my first twenty-seven years as a couples therapist I had seen how difficult and slow going it was for couples to change entrenched negative patterns. To be quite honest, it was personally frustrating so I began exploring creative methods to help couples. In 2010 I developed an alternative way to work with couples challenging many common beliefs about love and marriage accepted in our culture. I've found it helps me be far more effective as a couples therapist, and I've seen a radical difference with many couples showing more rapid and dramatic changes than I had ever seen before in my practice. It's been exciting to see the many transformations. For example, after just twelve sessions with one couple, the wife said:

> When looking back, I'm blown away. I can't believe how close I came to leaving him just before starting therapy. That would've been such a mistake, because we've now totally turned it around in a relatively short period of time. I really didn't think it was possible.

Both went on to share their feelings of happiness about the new depth of love, closeness, and absence of conflict not seen since early in their relationship. And now it's very common for me to see this kind of change in couples. More case examples will be offered in Section One.

Maximum Personal Responsibility for Change

This approach, called *Relationship Co-Coaching*, involves maximum personal growth and responsibility. Often couples want to find a therapist to "fix" the problems in the relationship—there's a natural tendency to blame each other.

This relationship model is different. It transfers the responsibility for the happiness of the relationship back to each of us individually. First, *what am I doing, or not doing* that is contributing to recurring issues and problems? The focus is redirected to how we can change our own self while sharing a mutual responsibility for relationship happiness. This stops habitual blaming.

It represents a fundamental shift in mentality that is critical to help a relationship move in a new, more positive direction.

Relationship Co-Coaching will challenge you on a personal level to examine your own relationship to break through negative behavior patterns and learn new, positive ones. And it will encourage you and your partner to unselfishly go out of the way to help each other feel deeply loved at the core of your being in the exact ways you both need.

This approach has helped many couples looking to fine-tune their relationships, overcome communication issues, and develop deeper love for each other. It has also helped couples with more serious problems break the destructive cycle of anger and conflict pushing them apart, and it has rescued others on the edge of divorce.

Not a Substitute for a Couples Therapist

Realistically it takes more than just a book if one has serious problems in a relationship. You'll have to put these ideas to work. But because it's so easy to fall victim to our own blind spots, one may need to see a good couples therapist for any significant problems. A professional can help a couple see the part that each one plays in what's going wrong in a relationship.

A Coaching Book

Welcome to this journey in learning how to improve your relationship. Thanks for being open to new ideas for your relationship. If you'll allow, I'll serve as your coach and guide for re-examining the beliefs that shape the way you interact with your partner, and offer relationship changing practices to achieve new a depth of happiness.

This book is also meant to be a potential resource for assisting couples therapists of all theoretical orientations in helping support their clients' growth. It can be particularly useful for help in overcoming blaming attitudes and resistance to change. To other therapists, let me just say I certainly don't claim to have all the answers but humbly offer these ideas for your consideration. In using this approach my effectiveness as a couples therapist has improved in a huge way. My life has been made much easier in working with couples, especially with difficult relationship cases. More importantly, from the feedback they give me clients seem to really appreciate the results. And interestingly, this approach seems to be in alignment with the hypothesized five common principles of change for successful couples therapy noted in a recent large-scale review of outcome research (see Appendix B).

This book is intentionally written in an easy-to-understand, conversational style, avoiding unnecessary fluff. Life is fast-paced and time is valuable; most people don't want to and shouldn't have to wade through several hundred pages to get at key ideas.

The emphasis here is on brevity using an experiential coaching format. Feel free to go at whatever pace you like. Some readers may want to read the book for the first time without stopping to do the exercises at the end of each chapter, coming back to them later; others may want to read one chapter at a time and keep up with the exercises as they go along. Either way, just imagine we're sitting across from one another having a casual, personal conversation and we'll take a look at how each of the book's ideas can be applied to your relationship. What you learn here can be applied to any relationship regardless of a couple's age, ethnicity, or gender.

So, where do we begin this exploration? Let's start with a greatly under-recognized problem in our society, the high statistical risk of any marriage failing.

Marriage Is High Risk: 50 Percent Ends in Divorce

Have you ever wondered why it is that the US, which is so highly developed economically, has a 40 to 50-percent divorce rate?[1] How can we as a nation enjoy so much prosperity, where most have access to cell phones, cars, large-screen TVs, entertainment, yet the very foundation of our culture—marriage—has roughly the same success rate as flipping a coin?

What would you do if you were offered a new job, but were told, "Oh, by the way, we have to tell you that your chances of achieving success in this particular position are only about 50 percent? In fact, you have an equal probability of failing, possibly being fired." Would you accept that job?

Probably not, most people would elect to look elsewhere for a position with more security.

However, everyone wants and needs love. So most people go ahead and take this incredibly risky plunge even though the statistics show that chances of success are so uncertain.

A Radical Viewpoint Regarding the High Divorce Rate

Are relationships and marriage simply too hard? Do people have too many issues? What exactly is the problem? Well, in my opinion society's lack of skills training and commonly accepted cultural beliefs set couples up to have problems and prematurely dissolve their relationships! Let's explore the reasoning behind this challenging statement.

We are still at a relatively early stage in the psychological and social development of our culture. Society has simply failed to place the necessary emphasis upon addressing the problem of divorce. We encourage a high level of achievement in the material sphere, but not in marriage.

Most of our educational focus and skills training have been confined to the economic achievements of life. Most of the emphasis in the educational system and business world centers upon the skills needed for economic advancement, not relationship enhancing interpersonal skills. These subtle interpersonal relationship skills do also contribute to one's ability to be successful in the economic arena of life; however here we'll focus primarily upon the skills to achieve a successful long-term romantic relationship.

Certainly society promotes development of general social skills reinforced through families, churches, temples, schools, and society at large. It's true that children are taught in a relatively informal sense how to get along with others and not be overly argumentative, selfish, or disagreeable. But what we're discussing here is a more disciplined, highly detailed relationship skills education. This involves a higher level of feedback and training regarding how we relate to others.

Examples of these interpersonal skills include body language, voice tone and inflection, language and word content, and many other aspects of the way a person communicates ideas, asserts needs, and handles difficult stressful situations—especially conflict. This involves a more intensive self-knowledge in how one comes across when relating to other people.

Actually there is considerable scientific research about many of the skills needed for relationships and marriage to be successful. But the problem is this information is not generally taught on a widespread level in our society. We will discuss some of the research findings most relevant to our discussion and our model.

Anticipated Resistance to Relationship Skills Training

We can anticipate that there might be many who'd respond with skepticism to the co-coaching model. Some might say, "Sounds great, but who's going to commit that kind of time, attention, and money to the development of such subtle interpersonal skills? We'd all have to go through extensive sensitivity training!" Well, that's exactly what needs to happen!

An Ideal Interpersonal Relationship Training

I had an early experience in my graduate school internship that was a great example of an educational institution providing precisely this type of interpersonal–social skills development. In fact, it had a great impact on my life, playing a major role in fueling my personal interest in the application of coaching and relationship skills training for marriages.

The University of West Virginia Medical Center offered a highly unusual training experience for all of its psychology, psychiatry, and social work graduate residents and interns. It was a unique experience not often offered for such trainees at other institutions. All of the psychiatry department faculty and multi-discipline graduate trainees met together once a week for what we called a "behavioral lab."

This was an incredible experience. Graduate students and faculty were on an equal footing, giving positive, as well as constructive feedback to each other. Any graduate trainee could express and, in fact, *did* express feedback to peers and even faculty.

This powerful experience was an impetus for my work in coaching business executives to help them employ a process of mutual coaching and feedback within teams. And this eventually led to the idea of applying reciprocal coaching to marriage and romantic relationships.

Why No Skills Training for Romantic Relationships?

Why doesn't society place more emphasis on developing the skills needed to ensure a happy relationship or marriage when there is so much emotional hurt resulting from separation and divorce? Some religious groups recommend pre-marital workshops or counseling, but even more extensive relationship education and training is needed. For just about any other function in society there's skill proficiency that has to be demonstrated in order to engage in that activity.

There are examples to be found all through society, including job-related work skills training, professional development, educational degrees, and more. For every grade level, there are requirements. For every employment position, there are educational requirements, as well as proficiencies to be demonstrated. Our society is quite strict in its emphasis on skills competency surrounding many functions of daily life. And this is a good thing. It allows for the smooth day-to-day organization of businesses, institutions, and government.

If you want to drive a car you have to take Driver's Ed, which includes completing a written exam and taking the road test with an examiner who evaluates your skill level to determine whether you will pass or fail. Think about it: If you want to do something as simple as drive a car, you have to demonstrate considerable competency before being allowed on the road.

Yet, for two of the most important and complicated societal life roles—marriage and raising children—absolutely no education or competency is required! What do you think would happen if you suddenly asked someone to step into the position of CEO for a company when that person lacked education, skills, or experience in business? How likely would it be that he or she would be able to perform the intricate skills required for that job? And how likely would it be that this business would be successful and still in existence over the long-term?

Divorce—An Urgent Social Crisis

Subsequently, it's no surprise that the divorce rate is so high given the current lack of education and training. It's as if failure in marriage is to be expected and socially acceptable. What exactly is happening? Society has largely ignored this social problem of divorce—it's an epidemic of monumental proportions! The 50-percent divorce rate tears at the very foundation of family social structure with devastating effects for everyone, especially children.

But most importantly, no one is doing enough about it. If 50 percent of the population were experiencing a disease, society would be highly motivated to do something about it. In actuality, we are experiencing a widespread *social problem* of even greater significance. The fact that society does not care more about this problem and try to remedy it leaves us with only one inescapable conclusion: We live in a society advanced in technology and material means, yet still primitive and underdeveloped in regard to teaching skills for success in romantic relationships and marriage.

Pervasive Beliefs That Sabotage Romantic Relationships

It's more than just the lack of skills training that is a significant factor behind the high divorce rate. Society's beliefs about marriage, not only in the US, but in other countries as well, are unrealistic and actually contribute to relationship problems. This book intentionally challenges these commonly held simplistic ideas. We need to engage in a deeper analysis of our relationships to identify those broadly accepted mainstream conscious and subconscious assumptive beliefs about romantic relationships and marriage that affect us in negative, harmful ways.

Beliefs shape the expectations of couples and influence each person's behavior toward the other. The way partners respond in their emotional reactions to problems, conflicts, and stressors encountered in a relationship are driven by these beliefs. The sabotaging effects of these cultural assumptions about relationships have been greatly under-recognized and insufficiently addressed in the field of marriage therapy.

A couple's decision-making can actually be influenced by these relationship expectations in such a way as to subtly move relationships toward dissolution, rather than sustained growth. This book helps you identify some of the most destructive beliefs that may be negatively impacting your relationship.

Given all these forces against us, is it really possible to have a very special, deeply loving, exceptional relationship? And is it sustainable over time? The answer to both questions is an unequivocal resounding yes!

Relationship Co-Coaching for Dynamic Growth

A new approach is offered here for love and romantic relationships challenging these harmful societal beliefs. It offers the missing education and training in powerful relationship skills to make your love flourish and last. There are four key principles of Relationship Co-Coaching that act interdependently; each depends upon the others and all work together to build and sustain love over time. Applying these principles on a daily basis can help take you and your partner to an entirely different level in your relationship, marked by deeper love and less conflict. This is what it's done for so many couples in my practice, and even for my own marriage!

1. Fulfill Your Partner's Love Needs

It has become overwhelmingly evident to me after years of practicing marriage therapy that there's one fundamental cause for all relationship problems: the unique *love needs* of one or both partners are not being met after repeated efforts to communicate these needs. Subsequently, deep-rooted feelings of frustration turn to chronic resentment and anger, which then result in emotional distance.

This is simple and intuitive. In this case the term *love need* is defined as a core need to feel deeply loved in a way unique to you and your personal preferences, ideals, and values in life. If your partner does not meet these love needs, unhappiness is inevitable.

The solution for so many relationship problems would seem to be so incredibly clear, why don't we make the purpose of romantic relationships and marriage to be the mutual fulfillment of love needs? Doesn't everyone deserve to be loved in the ways that they need to feel truly happy? Why do so many couples fail to do this for one another, something that would make them both so happy?

For you to be happier in your relationship, you will need to find out what are the unmet love needs that may be causing problems in your relationship. This book will help you do so. Any dissatisfaction in your relationship and areas in need of improvement will most likely be linked directly to those frustrated love needs.

Dr. Gary Chapman was one of the first to emphasize how important love needs are in *The Five Love Languages*, one of the most popular relationship books on the market. It helps readers discover their primary "love language" through self-assessment based upon a general classification of five need areas.[2] However, the problem with couples meeting each other's love needs goes beyond just knowing what they are.

When first developing Relationship Co-Coaching, I found that even when couples were helped to understand what each partner's love needs were, they still often failed to fulfill them. There was something missing. This book goes even further to examine those missing ingredients and what stops us from meeting those needs. We will take a more in-depth look at the complexities of love needs: how to most accurately assess them and why failure to meet those needs is so pervasive.

Most importantly, you'll learn to accurately identify your own love needs. In Principle One, we'll look at a process for developing insight about what your love needs are and how to articulate them. This will enable you and your partner to gain a better understanding of which unmet love needs may be an underlying cause for unhappiness and conflict in the relationship. This is a vital first step as you head down the path towards achieving deeper relationship happiness.

2. Identify and Change Negative Relationship Patterns (NRPs)

After identifying your love needs, you'll next learn how to overcome one of the chief resistances to fulfilling those needs, namely repeating negative relationship patterns (NRPs). Because most of us have never received any training in how to handle conflict, it's not surprising that we can get locked into repeating patterns of conflict, which can slowly erode the wonderful feelings of love bond and connection.

No one is perfect. Everyone enters into a relationship with subtle, deeply ingrained NRPs that inevitably collide and cause recurring conflict. Couples are not prepared to encounter negative aspects of their partners' behavior. They react with hurt and resentment, which can build up over time and seriously affect emotional closeness and feelings of love. Unfortunately, these patterns serve as a major barrier to being more open, receptive, and motivated to fulfill each other's love needs.

Couples walk into a marriage expecting they should have a lifetime of romantic happiness even though they have no skill in handling conflict. Wow, what a setup! So, how do we stop it from occurring, especially when it seems inevitable?

In Chapter Three, you'll learn about the top twenty most commonly occurring NRPs and have the opportunity to assess which ones are present in your own relationship. These patterns can easily become activated during discussions regarding competing needs of partners or perceived attacks to self-worth. In fact, it's exactly these NRPs that flare up during heated discussions regarding unhappiness over unmet love needs.

These are the principal drivers triggering and sustaining repeated cycles of conflict. It will be critically important for you to identify which NRPs are present in your relationship and take control of them. If you and your partner can take ownership for these behaviors and change them, it can stop the cycle of repeating conflicts.

This would free you to be more receptive and less selfish in meeting one another's love needs. However, it's hard for all of us to break out of these very entrenched patterns. But this is really only the initial step to overcoming conflict. Actually changing your NRPs will not be easy—old habits are hard to break. And it will take more than just self-awareness of your patterns. To do this, Principle Three is needed.

3. Reduce Conflict With Softly Specific Co-Coaching

Changing NRPs and stopping conflict of any type requires a new way of communicating about difficult relationship issues. When couples call me the first time I ask what problems they're having in the relationship and roughly 90 percent of the time they say "communication issues." They report trouble "listening" to one another and discussing issues without it ending in hard feelings or conflict. Or there may be silent conflict where both avoid talking, leaving uncomfortable tension. Either way, the buildup of hurt and resentment from recurring conflict can cause harm to feelings of fondness and romantic love.

Principle Three of Softly Specific Co-Coaching shows you how to communicate more effectively in a way that is more open, respectful, and reduces conflict. You'll learn how to say things assertively, yet in a manner that will allow your partner to remain receptive.

When using this method for giving feedback, a couple proactively seeks to change NRPs, meet love needs, and reduce everyday conflict. You make the commitment to always talk to one another in a nice, respectful way without any anger or verbal aggressiveness, *no matter what the circumstances*. You actively coach each other, giving respectful feedback when falling off track with behavior-change efforts. It becomes part of the basic expectation of being in a relationship. Because NRPs are ingrained habits and often difficult to change, this kind of mutual feedback is essential for creating change in a relationship.

After many years of seeing clients trapped in in these patterns, the realization finally came to me that most conflict is caused by two primary factors. We'll look at these two deeply ingrained recurring negative behaviors that underlie most every conflict you and your partner have had in your relationship. Most importantly, you'll learn how to use the six steps of the Softly Specific Co-Coaching process, which are designed explicitly to help you avoid these two behaviors and stop conflict. Many of the principles of the Softly Specific communication skills have grounding in recognized therapy practice and are in alignment with research.

Importantly, one of the primary goals of Softly Specific is to promote authentic communication and heal the deeper, more vulnerable emotions below the surface of anger, such as hurt, rejection, and sadness. This simple method helps reduce conflict and sustain a healthy relationship over the long-term. You'll have the opportunity to try out each of the six steps of the Softly Specific and practice them.

However, even after learning these co-coaching skills, you and your partner may still encounter an inner resistance to unselfishly meeting each other's love needs. Societal beliefs about love and relationships reinforce a self-centered concept of romantic love and marriage. That is why Principle Four is necessary to help you more fully embrace the idea of a relationship based on love that is more altruistic.

4. Seek Relationship Self-Actualization and Altruistic Love

Think about it: The first reaction of someone asked to unselfishly meet the love needs of his or her partner usually is often defensive or resentful. These feelings are reinforced by culturally transmitted deleterious messages about relationships alluded to earlier. A major shift in these programmed beliefs is needed to develop a new mindset, one that promotes a real interest in developing unselfish love for our partners.

That's exactly the purpose of Principle Four: self-actualization and altruistic love. Here, the term "self-actualization" is defined simply as the effort to achieve one's highest potential in life. Society's current beliefs place a number-one focus on occupational and economic achievement in life. What's missing in our culture is an equal priority upon also setting a life goal for achievement in a relationship.

It's important to note that one of the core principles of self-actualization is that a person actively seeks to go beyond just trying to meet material and emotional needs in order to develop altruistic (unselfish) love for others. Romantic love, as we now view it, is largely self-centered, based upon another person meeting certain requirements of physical and personality attraction.

If you can make this personal shift in thinking in your relationship, it places much greater importance on setting the intentional life goal of loving one another more unselfishly. This helps overcome any resistance to meeting your partner's love needs more fully. It opens up an entirely new aspect of fulfillment in life because loving unselfishly is immensely gratifying.

By using the power of all four principles working in cooperation and applying them diligently, it *is* possible for you to achieve new levels of love and happiness in your relationship!

Common Relationship Barriers and Sabotage

The book is divided into three sections: The first section offers a more in-depth presentation of the Relationship Co-Coaching model and its four principles, including case examples.

The second section of the book highlights common relationship barriers and sabotage factors, which can still hurt your relationship even if you are following the co-coaching model. We'll look at three sabotaging beliefs that can lead to premature break-ups. This second section also focuses on affairs and the resulting complications, as well as how to avoid them. Last, attention is given to stress, which can play a considerable role in harming relationships. We live in a perfectionistic, driven culture with everyone trying to do too much. This can be very detrimental to quality of life. We'll discuss practical strategies for managing stress more effectively in your relationship.

Love-Deepening Skills for Closeness, Affection, and Romance

And finally, the third section of the book deals with positive energy factors you can use to nurture the deepest love possible in your relationship. It starts with building in the four types of closeness needed for any relationship to thrive. Couples can easily forget to make their relationship a priority with busy, high-stress lifestyles. This can result is loss of emotional and romantic closeness. So even if you practice the co-coaching model, if you don't spend time connecting personally, your relationship may still suffer.

We'll look at the four primary ways that partners feel deeper love, closeness, and emotional connectedness. You will have the opportunity to assess which of these four areas of closeness and emotional bonding is in need of development in your relationship and how to make improvements in each area.

In addition, the third section emphasizes the importance of expressing positives, love affirmations, and romantic flirting. The reality is that couples often let their relationships grow stale. They don't engage in key behaviors that would help develop and strengthen their relationship. These actions are energizing skills to build and sustain a romantic relationship, making it last for years to come. This third and last section concludes with encouragement and support for you in the commitment to creating deeper love and an exceptional relationship.

Relationship Self-Exploration

Please feel free to use this book as a roadmap for self-discovery. Look at your own relationship to identify unmet love needs and negative relationship patterns. Learn new co-coaching communication skills to reduce conflict and embrace a new belief system for relationships based upon self-actualization and altruistic love. Identify and avoid potential barriers in your own relationship while injecting new, positive energy into your relationship with love deepening skills. Each chapter concludes with exercises to help guide you in determining which areas of your relationship are most in need of improvement.

So remain open to new possibilities. Sit back and let's begin this journey together and explore new ways to make your relationship a truly exceptional one!

The Relationship Co-Coaching Model for Dynamic Growth
1. Fulfill Partner's Love Needs
2. Identify and Change Negative Relationship Patterns (NRPs)
3. Reduce Conflict with Softly Specific Co-Coaching
4. Seek Relationship Self-Actualization and Altruistic Love

Section 1:
Co-Coaching For Dynamic Growth

Chapter 1

Challenging Prevailing Beliefs About Romantic Love and Marriage

We essentially have an entire population that's been mentally programmed from childhood onward with beliefs serving to consciously and unconsciously reinforce 50 percent of people divorcing!

Let's begin with examining the belief systems that influence and shape your expectations about relationships or marriage. These beliefs directly affect the way you react *to* and interact *with* your partner. It will be exceedingly helpful to determine the beliefs that may be working against you and your partner being successful in your relationship.

Your personal beliefs are largely influenced by society's commonly accepted conscious and subconscious beliefs about relationships and marriage, your parent's relationship and their interactions. If we don't first start with an analysis of the belief systems that may be currently influencing us, then we will be skipping a very important step. Developing insight about these beliefs and how they affect us is critical to achieving long-term relationship success.

In fact, if you are encountering significant problems in your relationships right now, these culturally conditioned beliefs may be causing you to feel prematurely pessimistic about that relationship, and your partner's ability to "be the right fit for you."

Exposing Destructive Societal Beliefs

One of the first and the most important voices to speak out about the negative impact of social attitudes and beliefs on marriage is Dr. Bill Doherty. He asserts that the culture of consumerism tends to tear relationships apart by moving couples away from long-term commitment. It promotes the idea of *tentative*, instead of *permanent* commitment. One is always looking for something newer and better. Partners tend to think they deserve better and have feelings of entitlement. As soon as problems are encountered, they begin to question the marriage and dissolve relationships far too easily. Doherty contends that many divorces are unnecessary.[3]

Doherty also makes the point that some therapists may reinforce this self-centered, consumer-like bias toward individual satisfaction instead of acceptance of family responsibilities and obligations. In fact, he says:

> I believe that there is a lot of unnecessary pain and unnecessary divorce created by incompetent therapists and by therapists who take hyper-individualistic approaches to marriage. In this view of marriage, marriage is a venue for personal fulfillment stripped of ethical obligations. And divorce is a strictly private, self-interested choice, with no important stakeholders other than the individual adult client. The result is in my opinion it is dangerous in America today to talk about your marriage problems with therapists unless you know what their attitude is and what their skill level is.[4]

This movement in the field of marriage to address the deleterious effect of societal beliefs on marriage is exceedingly important.

Harmful Romantic Beliefs

Doherty's focus has primarily been on the culture of consumerism and how it affects marriage. In this book, we explore the negative impact of society further through its underlying beliefs about romantic love and marriage. Let's take a closer look at these beliefs: What are they, why are they so pervasive, and most importantly—how may they be influencing you in your relationship?

Our guiding beliefs about relationships and marriage have come from subtle conscious and unconscious messages transmitted on a daily basis through our parent's relationship, television, films, the music industry, even religion. The most exciting, romantic mythologies of love and marriage are constantly being communicated because they are the most attractive and interesting. Unfortunately, this picture fails to communicate what is needed to sustain romantic feeling over the long haul.

Most everyone would agree they've been exposed to some of these cultural messages, including that you'll fall starry-eyed in love, experience wonderful, exciting feelings, get married and live happily ever after. And, if there are problems, two options are constantly communicated to us—an affair or divorce. How many movies center on the affair that leads to the unraveling of lives? Conversely, how many movies show couples avoiding this crisis through good communication and loving actions?

One may argue that most people understand there is a lot more to a relationship, requiring greater communication, understanding, and acceptance, however, there is comparatively much less emphasis placed on the positive development of these relationship behaviors.

Simplistic, Non-Growth Messages

After twenty-seven years of seeing couple after couple come into my therapy sessions with similar blaming attitudes and recurring patterns of conflict, I finally came to an important insight. Much of the difficulty in helping couples change relates directly to belief systems. Namely, there are fundamental problems in marriage that stem from self-limiting, non-growth expectations about relationships.

Underlying the many superficial messages regarding romantic relationships and marriage, there's one unifying, self-sabotaging belief. Most people believe they should not be asked to change themselves in a relationship. Subsequently, they're naturally resistant and become defensive. This pervasive *non-change* belief about romantic relationships sets couples up for problems and conflict.

For example, you've probably heard others say one or both of the following statements:

1. *Don't go into a relationship and ask your partner to change; just accept him/her for who they are.*
2. *You should just love me unconditionally and accept me for the way I am.*

These two commonly heard statements consciously and subconsciously reinforce the idea that relationships are static; that it's not okay to ask your partner to change. The broad-ranging repercussions of this belief—that it's not acceptable to ask a partner to change in a relationship—have not been sufficiently recognized in the field of marriage therapy.

Subsequently, when a person becomes unhappy or upset with the negative behaviors of his or her partner and communicates the feelings, the partner's first reaction tends to be one of defensiveness. Further, the partner being confronted typically interprets this request as controlling, and frequently reacts with anger or resentment!

How Relationship Problems Develop

Here's what happens in relationship and marital counseling sessions when there are more serious problems and far too much time has elapsed before seeking help: A couple initially comes in with one or both partners complaining they've tried so hard to fix the relationship, but there's been no improvement. One or both complain that the other has been unable to change upsetting behavior even after being asked repeatedly.

This negatively affects the couple's romantic feelings of love—they may not even be sure they're in love anymore. Or an affair may have occurred. At this point often they are questioning if they've picked the wrong partner and made a mistake. The presumed solution frequently becomes ending the relationship and over-focusing on the other partner as the problem. All of this is of course shortsighted.

This is a misguided approach steering both partners away from a more constructive process for solving the issues in the relationship. Also, one or both partners might now have considerable fear generated by the expressed concerns that there must be something wrong with the relationship. This keeps couples from looking more objectively at exactly what is happening developmentally and taking more constructive action.

Beliefs Reinforce Relationship Dissolution

Because of these non-change beliefs, the onset of normal, to-be-expected developmental problems in a relationship causes couples' thoughts to escalate quickly toward dissolution rather than the much better alternative of realizing they are at a predictable point in their relationship when negative patterns get in the way. There's no societal preparation or education. Couples aren't prepared to anticipate this absolutely critical developmental stage in a relationship.

It's not surprising then that finger pointing typically occurs. Most people don't know how to conduct a more thoughtful, personal self-analysis to find out how their own behavioral patterns, rather than just the partner's, are contributing to the conflict and lack of emotional connection.

This constant deflection from a more constructive approach can sabotage couples counseling. And, if these beliefs haven't been properly addressed upfront, it can also lead to one or both of the partners dropping out of counseling way too early.

Broad-Based Societal Education Needed

As long as simplistic, non-growth, beliefs remain unchallenged in society couples will continue to have unrealistic expectations about relationships. They may continue to be more inclined to divorce without ever putting in the work needed to try to save the relationship. We have an entire population that's been mentally programmed from childhood onward with beliefs serving to consciously and unconsciously reinforce the mentality that sustains the 50-percent divorce rate.

The specific plan to change these prevalent, self-limiting larger beliefs is beyond the scope of this book. However, let it be said that there needs to be a social education movement initiated as soon as possible; this affects the future emotional health and stability of our children. Fifty percent of all children born in our society go through emotional pain and upset when families break apart.

A great deal of importance is communicated in our society regarding the economy, political, and social concerns. It's time that everyone, particularly in the media, arts, religious, and political arenas give a much higher level of attention to this problem. There is also much potential for education about marriage relationships in business where relationship-related stress cost employers an estimated $6 billion[5] and a poll by CompPsych Corporation found that one in five employees say that "personal relationship issues" are their biggest distraction at work.[6]

We must build into our society's cultural messaging a new model of relationships and marriage. These new beliefs need to be cultivated and communicated. Couples should enter marriage with the expectation that there will be a need to discover and change negative behaviors. It needs to be understood that unselfish love, co-coaching, and effective communication skills are needed to sustain long-term fulfilling relationships.

Challenge Your Belief Systems

While the larger change in society may take considerable time, let's return to our primary objective: challenging your own belief systems. First ask yourself, have you or your partner been negatively influenced by these beliefs? Put aside any tendencies to be overly focused on blaming your partner. Rest assured, if you have feelings of hurt and anger, these are probably valid and justified. Your partner might indeed be engaging in behavior that does need to be changed. But instead of assuming change is not possible, I'm suggesting that there is a very positive solution to help you and your partner move your relationship to much higher levels of love, closeness, and passion.

The first, most important thing to realize is that you've been culturally conditioned with non-change oriented messages about relationships and marriage. This can predispose you to make negative value judgments about whether your relationship is right for you as soon as you begin to have any significant problems. So a new, more objective attitude about how to approach your relationship is needed.

And for couples with more serious problems considering whether to stay in the relationship, co-coaching can help you make a more objective, educated decision. There indeed may be situations where you may want to choose dissolution, but that will be discussed later.

Case Example:
I Don't Believe She Can Change

This client story illustrates how non-change societal beliefs can result in prematurely dissolving a relationship. One couple, Shane and Vicki, came in for an initial couples session, saying they'd been married for only five months but had daily conflict. More than half the time when they talked, it ended in a conflict. Just about once a month Vicki threatened to leave the new marriage.

Numerous times during the early stages of the therapy I had to challenge Shane's belief that Vicki wasn't able to change her verbally aggressive behavior. He was fixated on the idea that because of their frequent conflicts they weren't a good fit for one another.

In fact, after the sixth session the couple had a huge fight at home, and Shane asked Vicki to move out, which she did. He believed that her highly provocative, verbally aggressive behavior had crossed the line. This proved, in his mind, she was not capable of changing; he expressed the desire to divorce. However, I spent a good deal of time continuing to logically challenge him to give his wife and the relationship a chance since it was still very early in the process. He agreed to continue couples therapy and work on the relationship.

They committed to each of the four Relationship Co-Coaching principles, worked to change their negative relationship patterns, and consciously tried to meet one another's love needs. They are now proactive in using the Co-Coaching techniques on a daily basis for any minor issues, and use it an average of two to three times a week to discuss more important issues having the potential to become heated. After 20 sessions they completely turned their relationship around.

Importantly, both reported that their deep feelings of love and emotional connectedness returned. And they felt confident in their ability to maintain this turnaround in their relationship with the skills learned.

In discussing these changes made, the couple looked back on how things were in the beginning of their relationship. "For the three to six months before first coming in for therapy, it felt like we had irreconcilable differences, and both of us were 90 percent sure that we were going to divorce," said Shane. Since then, he's expressed appreciation for confronting him so assertively to stay in the relationship and continue the therapy.

If this marital therapy approach had not heavily challenged Shane's adamant non-change beliefs that relationships should not involve a lot of work and that a person cannot change, he would have in all likelihood terminated the relationship prematurely.

Understanding Developmental Stages of Relationships

Now, let's take a more in-depth, objective look at what happens developmentally in marriages over the natural course of time. This will give you a better understanding of what to expect in any long-term relationship. And it may offer insight into what's happening in your current relationship. Keeping it simple, there are three predictable developmental stages in relationships and marriage:

1. **Early romantic infatuation:** Being overwhelmingly *in love*. This entails all the fantastic excitement, deep feelings of emotional connection, and emotional security.
2. **Encountering Negative Relationship Patterns (NRPs):** We see the flaws and negative relationship patterns in our partner. Heightened resentment and anger occurs due to NRP conflict and love needs not being met.
3. **Deciding on a course of action:** What action do we want to take after dealing with the realities of stage two? Partners question whether to just accept things the way they are, try to improve the relationship, or leave.

For the purposes of this book, the primary focus here is upon stages two and three, offering proactive ways to improve your relationship.

Negative Relationship Patterns and Conflict

Let's start by focusing on the transition from wonderful stage one to the second stage; it's here where we encounter one another's negative relationship patterns. Progressively more serious tension and difficulties can develop in the relationship. This comes with the passing of time and other stressors in life. Everyone encounters this stage to one degree or another. The warning that signals this stage is the presence of more frequent conflicts, especially over seemingly unimportant issues. For some couples these relationship issues can gradually escalate to include more intense repetitive conflicts. When this happens, romantic feelings of love may begin to wane for one or both partners because of built-up resentment. This detracts from the feelings of romantic love for a partner. And this can, in more serious cases, progress to the point where partners begin to question whether they are still in love.

My Partner Is the Problem!

Further, the onset of significant relationship issues often triggers the frightening thought that maybe one has picked the wrong partner and made a major mistake. This causes one partner to focus on the other as the problem and consider dissolving the relationship. There is failure to engage in constructive analysis of how the behavior of both partners may be contributing to their problems and there are far better solutions than just discarding the relationship.

Deepening Love and Passion In Good Relationships

It may be that for many of you things haven't progressed to the severity described above. And perhaps you may fall into the 50 percent of married couples that don't divorce. You might be reading this book because you are aware that the depth of love, emotional closeness, and connectedness isn't what it was in the early stages of your relationship, and you want to rekindle those loving feelings. Your interest may be to just learn how to strengthen and keep alive the romantic love, passion, and excitement in your relationship.

If that's the case, don't worry. This book still applies to you. These developmental stages can still affect your relationship, even if you're not experiencing the severity and urgency described for couples with more serious difficulties.

Society's beliefs leave even higher-functioning couples feeling that they must accept diminishment of emotional, romantic feeling. The assumption is that it's something destined to happen, no matter what. However, this is absolutely not the case! There is, in fact, an almost unlimited potential to develop a deeply passionate, exciting love for your spouse even after years of marriage.

How My Own Marriage Changed

Let me share something with you personally. Until I developed this relationship model, my wife and I always had a very good marriage of 25 years with lots of love and affection. However, there had always been recurring conflict on occasion, which was not pleasant. After successfully using this new approach with many couples, I finally decided that I should practice what I preach in my own relationship!

We committed ourselves to using the Relationship Co-Coaching model. It wasn't easy and required substantial work; both of us had to change in big ways. But our relationship is in a completely different place now—better than it's ever been before!

Reformulate Self-Limiting Beliefs

How do you create change in your relationship? First, you and your partner must revamp your beliefs and expect the need for self-reflection. You need to each ask the question, *how are my own behavioral patterns, rather than just my partner's, contributing to the conflict?*

New Model for Love and Marriage

Reset your expectations for what it takes to be successful in any romantic relationship. Embrace the new premise that change and dynamic growth are, in fact, necessary to achieve the highest fulfillment in any relationship. This is in fundamental opposition to the prevailing non-growth concept of relationships. With this new belief system, if you experience pressure from a partner to change, this will help you react positively rather than negatively to the request. And if you are unhappy with certain aspects of your partner's behavior, you can now feel empowered to ask for what you need in the relationship.

With this shift in mentality, the Co-Coaching model can show you how to create the highest possible level of happiness in your relationship. We'll now take a more in-depth look at each of the four elements of this new approach in the next chapters.

Self-Exploration Exercises

Remember that you and your partner have been subject to the same cultural messaging. You've experienced constant bombardment reinforcing consciously or subconsciously these non-change self-limiting beliefs. You'll want to carefully look at how you may be influenced by any non-change assumptions made about your relationship:

1. What non-change beliefs are currently influencing me (or us) in the relationship?
2. How might they be negatively impacting me, or us?
3. In what ways would we like to see our relationship improved, or saved if problems are serious?
4. What changes would you like to see? Set specific goals for how you might want to take your relationship to a higher level of closeness and love.

Now you've explored how self-limiting beliefs might be getting in the way of your relationship and you're considering new possibilities and have set some initial goals for how you'd like to see your relationship improve. Next, let's explore what your underlying love needs are that need to be more fully met to move your relationship to a new depth of love and connection!

The Relationship Co-Coaching Model for Dynamic Growth

1. Fulfill Partner's Love Needs
2. Identify and Change Negative Relationship Patterns (NRPs)
3. Reduce Conflict with Softly Specific Co-Coaching
4. Seek Relationship Self-Actualization and Altruistic Love

Chapter 2

Relationship Problems Caused By Failure To Fulfill Unique Love Needs

Think about it: The biggest reason people are unhappy in marriage is that their core needs to feel loved in ways most important to them are not being met!

The next step for you is to find out what makes a relationship happy and successful. What became evident to me after years of practicing couples counseling is that one very simple, important factor is linked to relationship success: namely, the degree of happiness in a relationship ultimately relates to how well each person meets his or her partner's emotional love needs.

Given the fact you want to improve your relationship, it's likely that at least some significant love needs of yours are not being fully met. There may be some frustration with areas of your relationship that you want to make better. Surface issues might involve communication problems with too much conflict, lack of emotional closeness, loss of romantic feeling, or a variety of other concerns. However underneath these one will inevitably find frustrated love needs.

Unfortunately most people don't have a clear self-awareness of what their own love needs are or have great difficulty in articulating them. So it will be absolutely important for you and your partner to determine specifically what you each need to feel more deeply loved.

Relationship Problems Caused By Failure
to Fulfill Unique Love Needs

This isn't necessarily an easy process. You must first develop insight about your needs, communicate them in specific language, and then work with your partner to better meet each other's needs. This chapter will show exactly how to do this.

Sometimes there are other serious factors that obviously contribute to problems in a relationship and must be treated, such as drug and alcohol addiction, depression, or other mental illnesses. Even in these cases, this basic principle still holds true. Addiction or mental illness makes it more difficult, sometimes impossible, to meet the partner's love needs. But it's still the failure to meet those needs that makes the other partner unhappy. Here is the first key principle of the Relationship Co-Coaching for Dynamic Growth model:

Principle # 1:
Fulfill Partner's Love-Needs!

Each person, depending upon family upbringing, background, personality, and other factors, feels most deeply loved in ways unique to them. People are often very different in the way they need to feel liked, desired, and loved by partners. Everyone wants to know that there is someone who is always there, helping him or her feel safe, secure, and emotionally connected.

But what one person needs to feel deeply loved may be very different compared to another. It can be words verbalized, glances, smiles, body language, small gestures, shared interests, helping around the house, expressing appreciation, physical affection. It's very likely that partners will differ in what they need to feel loved. The mistake that many make in relationships is that they assume their partner wants their own love needs to be met in the same way they do.

It frequently happens that people fail to show love in the way that is most important to their partners. There's a tendency to see those needs as too different compared to one's own, not needed, or just too far outside of one's comfort zone. In addition, people tend to get caught up in the responsibilities, stresses, and problems of life. Habit patterns are deep-rooted and people find it hard to go outside of themselves. It's difficult to pay attention to the needs of another at the level required to really make that partner happy. At least this is an easy rationale for busy people who haven't made it a priority.

Unfulfilled Love Needs Cause Conflict

The biggest reason people are unhappy in marriage is that their core needs to feel loved in ways most important to them are not being met. They end up feeling frustrated and complain to their partner, who continues to fail at meeting those needs. This results in cycles of arguments and fights. The relationship becomes more vulnerable to deterioration in emotional connection and feelings of romantic love. In addition it may trigger non-change belief questions about the relationship being the right one.

One of the first exercises I do with couples is to ask them to independently think about and write down what they need to feel deeply loved by their partner. Then they share these needs with each other putting particular emphasis upon expressing the deeper, more vulnerable feelings of hurt, shame, and fear related to these needs not being met. This helps the couple reestablish a deeper emotional connection.

A heartfelt emotional healing can take place during this process. Additionally, we also probe more deeply into the specifics of what behavior partners would need to show one another to fulfill their love needs. And both commit to going out of their way to meet those needs.

Case Example:
Reigniting the Spark

The following case is an excellent example of how the healing power of meeting the love needs of a partner can quickly turn around a relationship, even one with problems extending over many years. Joe and Mary came in with the wife expressing the greatest amount of unhappiness with the marriage. Both complained that there was not much spark left in the relationship, which was reflected in the lack of sex. Mary complained that Joe had been emotionally absent for more than ten years, and he had still failed to connect with Mary emotionally in the way she needed during those years.

Exploration of Mary's love needs served to draw out the deeper feelings of immense resentment. For many years she felt neglected, emotionally abandoned, and sexually rejected. She was helped to express this to Joe, who was able to show substantial empathy and take ownership for his behavior.

In fact, he said that all of her feelings were valid and admitted: "I kind of want to get my way, I'm selfish. And I need to change." When Mary described his problems with listening to her needs, she said "it's his way or the highway, so I don't know if I can ever overcome this." In response, Joe said: "I acknowledge what she says. It may be that I'm a take charge person; I feel the need to dominate, but it doesn't work at home."

After sharing these deeper feelings, Mary was able to say that for the first time, she felt that Joe was really sorry for what he had done. She felt validated by him after expressing her feelings. Further, Joe committed to making big changes in his behavior.

In some situations when couples come in for counseling the relationship is obviously imbalanced with one partner unhappier due to their love needs having been so completely ignored and neglected. This was one of them. Subsequently, the priority of therapy is to first focus upon helping that person identify love needs and help the other partner to begin meeting those needs. After doing so, then therapy can shift to also helping the other partner's needs be met.

Interestingly, Joe's love needs were actually almost identical to Mary's. He also wanted to be emotionally closer in the relationship, to restore the "spark" with sexual intimacy, and have less conflict. And he knew that he was the one who needed to step forward to meet her love needs, thereby helping him fulfill his own.

Mary's complaints about Joe's behavior centered on his failure to give enough attention to their relationship:

Mary's five primary love needs:

1) To "feel equal"
2) Show more interest in spending time with me
3) Express more affection
4) Initiate romantic interest
5) Spend more time talking

As is always the case when uncovering love needs, the above were all expressed in generalized terms at first. After considerable explorative discussion, Mary was able to define the following specific behaviors she needed for these love needs to be met:

- To feel they were equal. In probing further, the behavior that she wanted to help her feel loved was for Joe to take more responsibility for helping out with cleaning in the home. In addition, she wanted Joe's support so she could consider developing a career now that the kids were older, even if this meant she would need to go back to school.
- Joe was to take initiative in setting up a date night once a week.
- Show interest in having sex more often.
- To snuggle on the couch before bedtime, showing more affection in general.
- To spend an hour together each night connecting in the family room with Joe fully engaged, not lost in self-absorbed thoughts.
- Joe would talk more and develop shared activities like going for walks, attending cooking class, etc.
- To explore spiritual interests together.
- To discuss their vision for the future.
- When they were at social events, Mary wanted Joe to hang out more with her, and socialize together rather than being apart from one another.
- Joe would continue to brainstorm about new, shared hobbies and interests to develop together.
- To socialize more together with friends in the neighborhood.
- Joe would take initiative to set up weekend activities for the kids and he would be more involved in overseeing these.

Joe committed to all of Mary's requests and met her love needs, which simultaneously served to meet his own. Marital counseling with this couple consisted of thirteen sessions. After 10 years of emotional distance and five years with no sexual intimacy, they achieved a total renewal of love and relationship closeness. Now they share more about their feelings, talk more every night, do more shared activities like walks and dates, and are exploring new interests together. The sexual relationship has been restored; they have sex once a week! Both say they're happier in the marriage now than since the very beginning of the relationship.

When the couple contacted me for brief consultation regarding children issues after one year and then again two years later, both reported the improvement continued at this same level.

Meeting Love Needs on Two Levels

Joe was particularly open and non-defensive. He very quickly went home and began to successfully fulfill all 12 of Mary's requests. This is an excellent example of how meeting a partner's love needs happens on two levels: emotional *and* behavioral. First, there is a profound emotional healing process that can occur therapeutically as it did for Mary. She shared deeper, more vulnerable emotions of feeling hurt, neglected, dismissed, and unloved. And she received heartfelt empathy from Joe; this helped kick-start the restoration of a much deeper emotional bond in their relationship.

Second, meeting the love needs of a partner also involves responding to behavior change requests and then actually sustaining the change, as Joe did.

Exploring The Deeper Meaning of Love Needs

As illustrated in the above example, exploring love needs often reveals significant emotional hurts. However, there may be an even deeper meaning to some love needs. For example, in a session with a client, she shared initially that her love need was for husband to help her "not feel insignificant." One outward expression of behavior she wanted was for her husband to be more available to take occasional calls from her while he was at work to discuss important matters that might pop up.

Recently she had called and asked him to leave work to help with an urgent situation. He declined and suggested a logical alternative. This left her feeling exceedingly hurt and "insignificant." She went on to say that if he had made the gesture to come and help her, "he would have saved me." In exploring the meaning of being "saved" she said the situation paralleled experiences in her childhood. She described a special connection with a sibling who literally saved her from being raped. He had always been someone emotionally there for her in a family with a physically absent father and an emotionally absent mother.

The insight came to her that she "needs someone who's always there for me," showing love in "actions and not just words." This insight helped both of them to much better understand the significance behind this love need.

So when you explore what your love needs are, take the time to think about what associations there might be to past experiences in your family or other relationships. However, don't think there must always be some kind of deeper significance behind your love need. A love need request should be taken just as it is—an opportunity to unselfishly love your partner in a way that's profoundly fulfilling for both of you.

Research on Emotional Engagement and Attachment

This approach of meeting the emotional love needs of your partner is intuitive and logically sound. There is also landmark research by Susan Johnson, PhD, regarding her Emotionally Focused Couples Therapy. Her research shows how responding to the deeper emotional needs for love and attachment in relationships improves therapy outcome. Couples showed a 70-to-73 percent recovery rate from marital distress in ten to twelve sessions of therapy and a 90 percent rate of significant improvement.[7]

Why Couples Fail to Meet Love Needs

If the road to greater happiness in any relationship is directly linked to how well a couple meet each other's love needs, you might be wondering why so many relationship partners aren't satisfying each other's love needs when it's so simple. More importantly, you may wonder why you and your partner haven't done a better job. What makes it so hard?

As mentioned in the introductory chapter, the idea of love needs is not new, yet the reasons for failure to meet love needs has not been more fully addressed. This book deals with the three root causes for why couples fail so often to fulfill each other's love needs and how each interacts with the other. In fact, if your love needs aren't being fully met right now, it's likely that one or more of these three factors are at play in your own relationship. So let's take a closer look:

1. Lack of clear definition of love needs

Because there is so little emphasis placed upon the idea of meeting love needs in our society, it's very common for couples to have difficulty identifying and articulating them. Usually those needs are communicated in the form of generalizations, such as not showing enough appreciation, not being respectful, not helping out around the house, and more. The problem is that each of these words will most likely mean entirely different things to different people.

In my experience, the process of fully exploring love needs may take at least one to two hours per partner to fully define their needs. Clients often have problems finding the words to define their love needs. It's hard to verbalize the specific behaviors they're looking for from partners. We are not taught to think about love and romance using behavioral language so it is naturally difficult for partners to convey their needs concisely in words. However, don't worry: This is what you'll-learn how to do at the end of this chapter.

2. Chronic hurt and resentment from repeated conflict

Chronic hurt and resentment from repeating conflict caused by negative relationship patterns make it difficult to even want to step forward to meet these needs. There is a direct link between love needs not being met and degree of conflict. Stored-up feelings of hurt and resentment from repeating patterns of conflict may cause a buildup of subconscious resistance.

It's natural to feel like we don't want to go out of our way to meet the needs of partners when feeling hurt or angry. The more negative feelings there are, the more resistance there is to act unselfishly towards a partner. It can be hard for one to show openness and interest in meeting each other's love needs if there are underlying negative feelings. This is especially true if we're upset over our own needs not being met! Thus, freeing up couples to better meet love needs may depend on how well they learn to handle conflict.

This is why the Relationship Co-Coaching process asserts that the first principle of love needs is inextricably tied to both the second principle of changing Negative Relationship Patterns (NRPs) and the third principle of reducing conflict. To be more specific, even if there's successful identification of love needs, harmful NRPs and conflict must be stopped, or at least managed more effectively. Otherwise, it's unlikely we'll open up enough to be more responsive to partners' needs.

3. Non-change, self-centered love beliefs
The third and last reason for love needs not being met is also equally important. Society's non-change beliefs and the tendency toward self-centered love work against a couple's motivation to unselfishly meet each other's love needs. Even if love needs are clearly defined and conflict reduced, there still may not be sufficient motivation to fulfill the needs of your partner. Life is busy, and we all have many things to think about and attend to on a daily basis.

Without a stronger, more intentional desire to go out of your way to unselfishly love your partner, it'll be hard to take the time to stop and identify your partner's love needs. And it will be equally difficult to remember those needs and act proactively to meet them every day.

What's necessary is we must make the conscious shift to unselfish love. This of course brings us to the Relationship Co-coaching's fourth principle of self-actualization and altruistic love, to be presented more in detail later. If it's not a life goal to achieve the highest level of relationship happiness and love unselfishly, then where's the motivation to make the extra effort on a daily basis to meet a partner's love needs? Hence, the first principle of love needs also depends directly on the fourth principle.

Meeting Love Needs: A Noble Goal, Challenging to Achieve

You have seen here how meeting love needs should be a fundamental goal for all romantic relationships, yet it's so hard to do. It's not as simple as just identifying each partner's love needs. The four principles of Relationship Co-Coaching act interdependently and all are essential for overcoming the resistances to meeting those needs.

This is what makes this book's approach to love needs so different. It emphasizes a direct, synergistic relationship exists among all four principles. Each adds power, building a support matrix of four interacting principles that energizes a relationship and moves it towards long-term success.

What Love Needs of Yours Are Unmet?

You may have some awareness regarding what your frustrated love needs are and have likely tried to communicate them to your partner, though perhaps with limited success. Don't worry if that's the case, and don't feel hopeless or assume your partner "can't change." What you'll learn here is that people are indeed capable of changing. It's quite possible your partner may be fully capable of learning to meet love needs that have remained frustrated up to this point.

The reason your partner has not been responsive to your needs is probably due to a number of factors as noted above and societal beliefs that one shouldn't have to change in a relationship. But equally as important, there probably has been a lack of clarity about those needs. This is a common problem—you may think you've been communicating for years what you want while in reality though, the specific behavior you're looking for hasn't been fully and clearly articulated.

For example, it's typical for couples to make generalized statements like "you don't listen to me," "show appreciation," "respect me," "emotionally connect," "value my opinion," etc. However, these simplified complaints are not enough. Most couples don't realize the degree of specificity that's been missing when conveying their needs.

Unbiased Self-Discovery of Love Needs

Let's first start with making sure your love needs are accurately identified. What I've found particularly important in exploring love needs is to avoid using a pre-selected limiting set of categories from a list of common love needs. Providing a list may seem convenient yet divert from your own process of insight and self-discovery. It's better for partners to rely on self-awareness to determine what they really need to feel loved without any bias or outside influence. The definition of what love needs are and the process for discovering them is simple. Just ask yourself the following question:

What do I need to feel deeply loved by my partner in the relationship?

The answers you get to this question will reveal your love needs, so just watch for what comes into your inner awareness. Some of these needs may be already met, and if so, that's ok. It's helpful to identify those things your partner *is* doing that *do* help you feel loved. Most importantly, it will help you determine those things your partner is *not* doing, or not doing enough of, that is causing you to feel frustrated in the relationship.

But be careful: the words used to describe general love needs—such as "appreciation" and "respect"—may mean different things to different people. Each generalized need must be defined further regarding the specifics of what it means for that person individually. So ask yourself the following questions:

What would this need look like if it were being met?
How does my partner not meet this need right now?
In what way is she or he or he meeting this need already?

Give specific examples for each of the above questions. It is also important for you and your partner to actively engage with one another in this discovery process. Share insights; ask each other the above questions and write down verbatim the responses.

Another reason for not using a pre-set list is that it may set the tone for discussion to remain only at the behavioral level, rather than going to experiences of deeper emotional healing regarding hurt feelings because of unmet love needs.

Examples of Exploring Love Needs

One couple, the woman in her late 60s and the man in his early 70s, came in for couples work. Both had been divorced and had children from those earlier marriages. Below are the primary love needs they initially expressed. Note the wording they used to express their needs is in the form of generalizations, and that the love needs for the wife are particularly ambiguous and lacking definition.

Primary Love Needs:

>*His:* Frustrated from the total abandonment of all touch
>*Hers:* To show interest in building a relationship

The wife felt that she had been very clear in communicating to her husband for years what she wanted with the statement of "showing interest in building a relationship." However, it wasn't until we explored what she meant by this generalized wording and broke it down into the four specific behaviors detailed below that her husband understood for the first time what she really wanted. This shows how subjective and idiosyncratic the meaning of words can be to different people and how it's important to articulate in specific language what one's love needs actually are.

Her specific love-need behaviors for "showing interest in building a relationship:"

1) Talk to me nicely with no sarcasm or putdowns.
2) Be positive, happy in your mood, and don't be so easily upset, angry or irritable.
3) Be open and honest:
   a. When I ask a question give a direct response without any "white lies."

4) Actually listen:
    a. Don't interrupt me in the middle of a sentence. If you do, then apologize and ask me to continue. Show true interest in what I am saying, and try to remember it.

His specific love-need behaviors for "abandonment of touch:"

1) Nonsexual physical affection:
2) Be comfortable in receiving my attempts at physical affection and touch; please give physical affection to me.
3) Heal and get over your anger:
4) Let go of your anger, the same as you do with the children when you get mad at them. Stop making assumptions of malicious or negative intent about the things I do or say; for example, the only reason you want touch is that "you're wanting sex", etc.
5) Don't be defensive.

After probing more deeply the interaction between their two love needs, she said the reason for the lack of physical affection and sex in the relationship is because of the way he "treats her and talks with her." This illustrates how frustration in love needs of one partner directly affects willingness to meet the needs of the other partner.

This is a good case in point for how it takes some time and exploration to draw out the specifics of love needs. Most of us need time to think about what our loves needs actually are and to put them into precise wording. Unfortunately, the wife in this case made the mistake that many make in assuming that a partner actually knows what is meant when frustration is expressed about a love need not being met. From her perspective, her words "to show interest in the relationship" were self-evident; she expected her partner to know exactly what she meant, even though it was not at all really clear to him.

Here's another example of exploring the specifics of love needs. In working with another couple, a partner described one of her love needs as "showing interest in me." Now, these words could mean a variety of things to different people. Further discussion defined this need as "asking questions of me and e-mailing as well as talking to me about things; I want a connection—a true interest in getting to know me." Although her husband had heard the complaint before of "not showing enough interest," it wasn't until hearing this more explicit definition that he knew what she was really talking about. Only then was he able to take specific action.

This is a common occurrence. Couples may express frustration—often over many years—to their partners using generalizations, or words that hold a subjective meaning but are not definite or understandable to their partner. There may be a huge gap in the actual understanding of the specifics of what the love need is and the behavior change needed to meet it.

So, let's explore right now what you and your partner need to feel more deeply loved in your relationship. Then, you can share those needs with one another and begin meeting them! Follow the specific steps in the Self-Exploration Exercises.

Self-Exploration Exercises

1) Ask yourself what you need to feel deeply loved by your partner. In what specific ways have your love needs been met and in what ways have they not been met? Where would you like to see improvement? Do this self-examination independently from your partner and write down what you discover.
2) Ask your partner to independently identify his or her needs to feel deeply loved. How have those love needs been met, how haven't they been met, and where would your partner like to see improvement? Ask him or her to write down those needs.
3) Come together and share your love needs. Help your partner try to get as specific as possible in defining the what, when, where, and how of each need. Ask the following three questions of one another:
   What would this need look like if it were being met?
   How am I not meeting this need right now?
   In what ways am I fulfilling this need already?
4) Take ownership for discovering and writing down the details of how to meet each need of your partner. <u>Define the specific behaviors for each need</u>.
5) Encourage your partner to share any hurt feelings surrounding these needs not being met. However, make sure that you show empathy, and sincerely apologize without any justification or defensiveness (see Softly Specific Co-Coaching steps in the next two chapters).

6) Finally, place the written love needs for your partner someplace where you can be reminded of them every day until you've completely memorized them. Make the commitment to meeting those love needs for one another every day. This is the most important step—taking action to consistently meet those needs!

You've now clearly identified your love needs *in very specific language*. Your first step is now completed. However, as noted earlier, this is just our starting point. There are other serious interfering factors that can get in the way of you and your partner mutually meeting love needs, such as repeating conflict and self-centered love. Let's start first with learning how to stop conflict from happening in the next several chapters!

The Relationship Co-Coaching Model for Dynamic Growth

1. Fulfill Partner's Love Needs
2. Identify and Change Negative Relationship Patterns (NRPs)
3. Reduce Conflict with Softly Specific Co-Coaching
4. Seek Relationship Self-Actualization and Altruistic Love

Chapter 3

The Inevitable Collision of Negative Relationship Patterns (NRPs)

NRPs erupt in particular after buildup of frustration and unhappiness from needs being communicated to partners who then fail to meet them.

One of the chief contributing factors as to why partners fail to meet each other's love needs is repeating conflict. Are there any "communication issues" in your relationship? Is there conflict or unspoken tension you want to reduce for a more relaxed, loving relationship? If you're like most couples, your answer to both questions will likely be *yes*. This chapter and the next two will help you learn new, highly effective skills to improve your communication and reduce conflict. Let's first start with the most common negative behaviors that create conflict.

Principal #2:
Identify and Change Negative Relationship Patterns (NRPs)

The term negative relationship pattern (NRP) is defined here as any negative behavior that hurts the relationship and damages emotional closeness or loving feelings. All couples bring at least some negative patterns to a relationship and these serve as barriers, triggering arguments. Couples then can get caught up in the conflict and resentment surrounding their NRPs and then fail to meet one another's love needs. In your relationship it will be imperative to identify what NRPs are causing harm and triggering conflict.

We are all imperfect people. The inevitability of facing the imperfections of our partner needs to be part of the expectation we have for relationships and marriage—the person we are so in love with has shortcomings, foibles, maybe even faults. And these are likely to be upsetting to us and generally we are unprepared for this disappointing reality.

In the initial stage of romantic love, there is something truly amazing! We experience emotionally high feelings. More importantly, we've all come to expect this from what we've seen on TV, in movies, in novels, and frankly, even from our own experiences. What a great feeling, isn't it? This exhilaration, however, fades over time as you encounter the less-than-positive, even selfish or negative, behaviors of your partner.

In the busyness of life with all its stress, our worst behaviors can easily come to the attention of those who love us. These behaviors likely were present during the earlier stage of romantic feelings, but perhaps deemphasized or simply ignored due to the wonderfully addictive feeling of being "in love." It's perfectly natural not to give much attention to these flawed aspects of our personalities during the initial stage of the relationship.

This romantic high feeling may last for anywhere from a few weeks to several months or even several years for some couples. It depends largely upon the degree of stress in life. For example, job stress, working long hours, work travel, or having children or a blended family can each move the relationship forward quickly into the reality stage. Negative behaviors can suddenly become increasingly evident. Your partner's issues may have become much more pronounced due to stress and the progression of time. There comes a point that you can no longer ignore problematic NRPs. More frequent tension and conflicts may occur, causing either a decline in your feelings of romantic love or more serious problems in your relationship.

Couples don't anticipate the natural occurrence of NRPs. Most wait far too long before doing anything about the repeating patterns of conflict. On average, couples wait six years before seeking help for marital problems![8]

Anticipating the Clash of NRPs

In this new model for relationships and marriage, we *build in* the expectation for the inevitable collision of NRPs. It will naturally occur in all relationships and we all have to expect this and be prepared for it. Let's take a look at some of the common NRPs. Below are the top 20 most common complaints I hear from couples about spouses when coming to see me for counseling. They are presented in the typical language a client uses when complaining about a partner. Do you recognize any of these in your relationship, especially during stressful or difficult conversations? My guess is you'll likely find one or more of the above behaviors that apply to you and your partner.

1) Problems with controlling temper and anger
2) Doesn't really listen to me during conversation
3) Interrupts me when I'm talking
4) Bossy and too pushy
5) Always thinks and acts like he or she is right
6) Too defensive
7) Verbally aggressive (sarcastic, raising voice, gruff, belittling, swearing, etc.)
8) Never apologizes for anything
9) Always needs to win in arguments
10) Easily frustrated, impatient, irritable, crabby, or terse
11) Complains, blames, or accuses too much (using global generalizations and negative judgments)
12) Too emotionally reactive and easily upset
13) Overly critical
14) Overly controlling
15) Overly passive, doesn't speak up with opinion, passive aggressive, punishing with emotional distance, silence, or other consequences
16) Not well organized, tolerant of too much clutter, or trouble following through in getting things done when promised
17) Doesn't show enough appreciation

18) Lies in order to avoid conflict or out of fear of disappointing others (white lies)
19) Doesn't share enough with me about the day and the things that happened
20) Emotionally disconnected and always working on the computer/electronic devices, or constantly texting at night instead of spending time with me

After introducing to couples the idea that NRPs will naturally occur in any relationship, I've found it much easier to help them work through their blaming and defensiveness. It's important to understand this is a part of the natural developmental process of relationships. Each of us will always have to face NRPs—our own and our partner's. Without this preparatory component, I've found couples often stay stuck in defensiveness, anger, and blame.

NRPs Linked to Unmet Needs

These NRPs are damaging to a relationship in two ways. First, these are negative behaviors that frustrate and turn off each partner, creating conflict. Second, these complaints also often reflect a failure to meet the deeper love needs of a partner.

Thus, NRPs and unmet love needs often overlap. For example, let's consider #13: being overly critical. One person being too critical can result in a failure to meet the love needs of a partner who has a desire to be acknowledged and affirmed in self-worth. The result may be feelings of hurt, rejection, and hopelessness. Over time it can be perceived as a direct attack to self-esteem, even triggering deep-rooted fears of abandonment. One might then feel it necessary to leave the relationship to avoid further assaults to self-esteem.

This is an example of how NRPs often represent the surface aspect of deeper conflicts over emotional love needs not being met. NRPs erupt in particular after buildup of frustration and unhappiness from needs being communicated to partners who fail to meet them. Exploring NRPs can become the window for discovering underlying love needs that one is failing to fulfill.

Case Example:
Don't Touch Me; I'm Dead Inside

The following client situation demonstrates very well how NRPs erode positive feelings of romantic love and emotional connection when left unaddressed for years. More importantly, it shows how changing these patterns can completely rekindle a relationship.

Jason and Andrea are in late middle age. Married for thirty-five plus years, they were to the point of severe estrangement. Jason was the pursuer in the relationship wanting to spend time with Andrea. He desired more affection and sex. But, she said, "I don't want him to touch me. I'm dead inside." Andrea wanted more "alone time" rather than closeness with Jason.

Both indicated a very high level of conflict in the relationship. They would argue about the "stupidest little things," fighting over who was right or wrong. They openly admitted to a pattern of both thinking they're the one who's right. Andrea complained that Jason was exceedingly defensive, raised his voice, and got angry too often. Jason felt that Andrea didn't express enough appreciation and that her wanting to spend time alone showed she didn't care for him.

The top three NRPs identified for Andrea were not showing enough appreciation, not sharing enough of herself, and always acting like she's right. Jason's top three NRPs were having a problem with anger and temper, acting like he's always right, and being defensive. The couple committed to changing these NRPs and co-coaching one another for slip-ups.

In addition, they identified love needs. Andrea's primary love needs were for Jason to be supportive of her spending time alone or apart from him, really listen to what she had to say and remember it, spend time in trying to understand her needs, stop being so defensive, and be willing to apologize. She had no romantic feelings for Jason because he was far too defensive and not supportive of her spending time alone. Subsequently, she complained of having no sexual feelings. Sexual intimacy had occurred only four to six times over the previous year.

Jason took ownership for his problems in listening and worked on being less defensive while being supportive of Andrea taking time for herself. Both worked hard on changing their NRPs and used the Co-Coaching method presented in next chapter. They were able to greatly reduce their constant arguments and stop the feeling of *I'm right and the other person is wrong*.

After sixteen sessions the couple reported they had taken control of their NRPs and reduced conflict from its everyday occurrence to now, on average, only twice a week, which they were able to more quickly resolve. They estimated the intensity of the conflict now was reduced by approximately 80 percent. And, importantly, they were now having sex about once every two weeks. Andrea summed up the change in their relationship in this session by saying,

> Before we started therapy there was underlying conflict all the time. I just didn't like him. We were just living together with no sexual intimacy. Anytime we talked about anything, he'd just get defensive, angry, and loud. I couldn't take it. Now both of us have learned to think and not react in discussing things. He's worked on his voice tone and worked very hard at not being defensive. We had kept our distance and I avoided him. We didn't talk. We were dead. There was nothing there in the relationship for me. We were just living together with great distance, and I wanted distance in the relationship. I felt no romantic or positive emotional feeling. Now, I feel much more positive and have loving feelings. I now know that sex is 95 percent emotional and 5 percent physical. I was dead and thought I could be a nun! Now, the sexual feeling is back. And I just don't need as much alone time now.

Men Sharing Power Have Happier Marriages

After years of marriage counseling, I've found that often the husband has failed to listen and be more sensitive to the needs of his wife, as in the above case example. In fact, the wife is more likely to be the most vocal in initially expressing unhappiness about the husband's NRPs.

Research shows that the ability of men to be "influenced" by their wives directly relates to a couple having a happier marriage. One of the pioneers in research on successful marriages is John Gottman, PhD. In a long-term study of 130 newlywed couples, Dr. Gottman found that those husbands who in the first few months of marriage allow their wives to influence them had happier marriages. More importantly, they were less likely to divorce than men who resisted their wives influence. In fact, men unwilling to share power with their partner had an 81 percent chance of having their marriages self-destruct. [9]

Gottman indicated that women were much more likely to allow their husbands to influence decision-making. Women took their husband's opinions and feelings into account. Unfortunately many men do not respond in the same way. So, men who aren't very willing to share power or listen to the needs of their partners and who also have a significant number of NRPs may tend to have marital problems. They must learn to become better tuned into their partner's love needs and act to fulfill them.

NRPs Direct Cause for Relationship Conflict

Let's go into a little more detail about some of the more prominent NRPs. The most frequently encountered behaviors in couples counseling are the first 14. One or more of these behaviors tend to be present in most every relationship conflict. Most couples seeing this list for the first time indicate that they recognize many of these first 14 NRPs in their own relationship.

The importance of these first 14 NRPs is that they all are verbally *aggressive* influencing and defense behaviors. This means that all serve the purpose of trying to help emotionally support or protect oneself. These are efforts to influence others to get love needs met or in defense of one's self-esteem from perceived attacks by others.

If you look at these particular NRPs more closely, you'll see that it's really the presence of one or more of these 14 behaviors that is the direct cause for most conflict. Unfortunately it seems human nature for people to fall easily into these behaviors. Each one, when expressed, has an extremely high likelihood of triggering an equally aggressive backlash from the recipient of that behavior.

These 14 NRPs are disguised, highly charged powder kegs. They are landmines that will sabotage effective resolution of any issue. In fact, if you want to increase the likelihood of any discussion turning into a conflict, then just introduce one of these NRPs.

If we never became defensive, raised our voice, failed to listen, interrupted, became blaming or accusatory, then there would never be any conflict! Discussions over competing needs and differing opinions would proceed smoothly, with great respect shown for one another, without any aggressiveness.

So why are these 14 NRPs so universally present in relationship arguments? Perhaps it is just human nature, a natural defensive stress response to perceived threats to self-esteem. However, in my opinion, one of the major reasons is that we're not taught how to handle conflict in any other way.

Aggressive Personalities Are Role Models

We mainly learn how to handle conflict through social modeling. We observe the interactions of our parents, authority figures, friends, colleagues, and bosses. Their bad examples are modeled, often subconsciously. We also learn from TV and movies. These 14 NRPs are seen in many instances as being socially acceptable simply because we're not taught better ways of handling conflict.

Further, society actually places a premium on certain aspects of being aggressive. For example, strong dominant personality tendencies receive considerable positive reinforcement in our culture. However, many of those same people who display positive traits of strength encouraged in society are prone to demonstrate these 14 negative behaviors.

Some of these valued positive personality characteristics and behavioral tendencies in our culture may include strongly communicating one's opinion or thoughts, self-confidence, ability to take action, and inclination to take leadership roles. Hence, such people often are placed in dominant employment positions. They are seen as knowledge experts and leaders taking on important organizational work.

So when these same strong personalities handle conflict in public situations using any of these 14 NRPs, they become our default social models. This is where we learn how to resolve conflict. It's like we are going to relationship school every day when watching parents and authority figures demonstrating both positive and negative behavior patterns.

NRPs Reinforced in the Business World

Let's delve a little more deeply into this social modeling in the business arena. Many of these 14 NRPs are still acceptable in organizational settings where other like-minded individuals believe these behaviors are necessary to achieve results or to improve performance. For example, dominant, pushy, impatient, and verbally aggressive negative behaviors are often tolerated or even preferred by some leaders, if they get results.

I've observed the acceptability of these 14 NRPs in coaching executives in business. Many higher-level executives and their companies advocate leadership traits of empowerment, caring and respecting employees, and openness to the ideas of the employees; however, when dealing with a poor-performing employee or poor financial results, leaders often tolerate the use of verbally aggressive behaviors. This can be displayed in a more overt form of aggressive behavior or it may be a more subtle form, such as showing impatience, irritability, and frustration with others (NRP #10).

Authoritarian Leadership Still Permeates Business

While many CEOs and executive leadership teams say they have a very open, caring culture, surveys of employees show otherwise. Bosses may see their company as being very caring and open while their employees do not. Dov Seidman, CEO of LRN, a company that helps businesses develop ethical corporate cultures, contends that the way a company does business is extremely important. Seidman commissioned a study by the Boston Research Group, *The National Governance, Culture, and Leadership Assessment,* in which employees in thousands of American firms, from every level in the corporation, were surveyed with these results:

> It found that 43% of those surveyed described their company's culture as based on command-and-control, top-down management or leadership by coercion—what Mr. Seidman calls "blind obedience." The largest category, 54% saw their employer's culture as top-down, but with

skilled leadership, lots of rules and a mix of carrots and sticks, which Mr. Seidman calls "informed acquiescence." Only 3 percent fell into the category of "self-governance," in which everyone is guided by a "set of core principles and values that inspire everyone to align around a company's mission."[10]

This research study indicates it's still a pervasive problem that many leaders continue to manage in a more authoritarian, aggressive style. And why is this relevant for our NRP discussion? This management style typically reinforces the acceptability of resorting to these 14 NRPs in organizational work settings, *and this ultimately can carry over to romantic relationships.*

Aggressive Parenting Style Reinforces NRPs

Parenting methods commonly acceptable in society start the early reinforcement of these same 14 behaviors. As children we learned from watching our parents display certain NRPs when they were frustrated or unhappy with our behavior, or with one another. Cultural beliefs regarding parenting provide similar rationale. When a child is acting up or not obeying, then it's okay, and perhaps even culturally acceptable to use these behaviors. Sure, most parents know it's better not to use physical punishment, but unfortunately there still is liberal use of verbal aggressive behavior when dealing with frustrations relating to children's behavior. It's viewed as perfectly okay to elevate one's voice, even yell, and show impatience, irritability, or anger towards one's children.

This parenting style of using verbal aggressiveness leaves children feeling disrespected, humiliated, and resentful which may result in them more prone to want to rebel in kind with aggressiveness. In fact, this is supported by research showing that harsh verbal discipline instead of helping adolescents actually harms them. A recent study of 976 two-parent families and their children found the use of harsh verbal discipline at age 13 predicted an <u>increase</u> in adolescent conduct problems, as well as depressive symptoms.[11]

Parents often have a hard time understanding how expressing frustration and impatience with their children is not a desirable strategy to help correct behavior. When parents say it's too hard or unrealistic not to speak that way, I challenge them: *Would you ever talk to your boss that way?* And they reply no. This answer, I tell them, proves they *do* have the control and the ability to speak nicely; they've just grown accustomed to talking this way to children because their own parents did and society has reinforced the behavior.

I further ask parents: *Would you want your boss or coworker to show that kind of impatience, irritability, or terseness with you?* Of course, their response is that they would not like it. So why should your children like it and respond any differently? Instead, I offer them an alternative parenting strategy that uses no verbal aggressiveness, is always respectful to the child, and is highly effective.

There is an implied societal assumption that because children are smaller, less developed, even less powerful, it's okay to talk to them showing impatient frustration using verbally aggressive language. The important point here is that parenting styles using these kinds of behaviors teach children from an early age how to respond in adult relationships. They learn how to react negatively in the *same ways*, especially when feeling stressed or frustrated with someone else.

NRPs Erode Love

The problem with showing frustration, anger, or any kind of verbally aggressive behavior is that, quite simply, no one likes to be the recipient of it. It doesn't matter who you are, whether you're an employee hearing it from a boss, or a child on the receiving end from a parent, in either case one feels disrespected. Using any one of the 14 NRPs with anyone you're romantically involved with has every possibility of making your partner feel hurt, resentful, and inclined to respond with one of their own NRPs.

In analyzing this developmental process further in which NRPs collide with each other, negative behaviors tend to eat away at a partner's feelings of romantic love. Of course this is particularly true for the one who is the recipient of the negative behavior. As time goes on, more and more resentment can be tucked away in the subconscious mind—bitter feelings build up. Deterioration in feelings of love and affection can quickly begin to occur.

Society's cultural beliefs regarding the acceptability of subtler aggressive behaviors in both organizational management settings, in parenting, and relationships serve to psychologically condition and program these behaviors into the very fabric of human interaction at practically every level. It's no wonder that these behaviors are commonplace in marital interaction. Subsequently, some of these 14 NRPs may have become an ingrained part of the conflict pattern with your partner.

Watch Out for Feelings of Hopelessness

It's important that you understand how common it is for these NRPs to spring up in your relationship. When serious NRP conflict occurs, it's important not to make premature assumptions. Don't assume that a lessening of your positive feelings for your partner means that you are no longer in love or he or she isn't right for you. What you must do is reframe the way that you've been looking at your relationship. In particular, be careful: You may fall victim to beliefs that it should be easier and shouldn't require this much work. You need to understand that it absolutely does require this much work.

But here's the most important thing to remember: Don't be so afraid as you enter this stage of a relationship, or realize you've been there for a while, maybe even a very long time. If you feel the inner frustration with your partner and if any of your loving or romantic feelings of fondness or endearment for your partner have been negatively affected, don't react prematurely! Don't assume that yours is a hopeless situation or that this may not be the right partner or marriage for you. Instead, take a very positive attitude. Know that encountering your partner's NRPs is actually a very normal, expected part of any relationship. Take a more educated, objective approach. Analyze what NRPs are at play in your relationship. Let's find out what they are through the next exercises, and then discuss them with your partner and both make the commitment to changing your behavior.

Self-Exploration Exercises

Take the time to look at the list of 20 NRPs to assess which ones are present in your relationship:

1) Which ones do you see in yourself? Conduct a self-assessment.
2) What are your partner's NRPs? Which ones bother you the most?
3) How have you dealt with any feelings of hurt and resentment accruing from your partner's NRPs?
4) Both you and partner sit down to openly share NRPs with one another.
5) Share with one another how your feeling of emotional connectedness and romantic love been affected by the clash of NRPs in your relationship.
6) Both of you commit to taking ownership for your NRPs and giving needed feedback when slipping up (using coaching methods in next chapters).

After going through the above exercises, you have now identified which NRPs are the biggest problem for you both. You also have a much better understanding of how these behaviors drive conflict and why they're so hard to change. In addition, both of you have taken ownership and are committed to changing NRPs. It's likely that your next question, however, is how you can actually change these NRPs and reduce repeating patterns of conflict in your relationship. Well, the next chapters will show you how.

The Relationship Co-Coaching Model for Dynamic Growth

1. Fulfill Partner's Love Needs
2. Identify and Change Negative Relationship Patterns (NRPs)
3. Reduce Conflict with Softly Specific Co-Coaching
4. Seek Relationship Self-Actualization and Altruistic Love

Chapter 4

Co-Coach Yourselves—Break the Cycle of NRP Conflict to Deepen Love!

One of the primary purposes of Relationship Co-Coaching is to help couples gain control of and change harmful conflict to support them in feeling safer and more secure in sharing deeper feelings.

Finding out what your NRPs are is an important step, but now the real work begins; now you need to learn how to actually change those NRPs. This one of the biggest challenges we face.

Often NRPs are fallback behaviors popping up to the surface when communication goes badly, fueling conflict. When couples say they have "communication problems" it typically involves the following: One partner may express some concerns or important feelings to the other, but feels frustrated when he or she becomes "defensive," "doesn't listen," "interrupts," or gets "angry" (all NRPs). Then, a back-and-forth disagreement ensues, escalating rapidly. Does this sound familiar for your relationship?

This seems to be the universal cycle for conflict—hard to stop once it takes off. Or *covert conflict* results in uncomfortable silent tension from buildup of negative feelings. Whether overt or covert, too much conflict is harmful. It saps the positive-romantic feelings and vitality from your relationship.

Let's explore how you can learn to stop conflict. First, we once again start with society's failure to provide relationship education. No one ever warned us that after the early phase of romantic infatuation, even in really great relationships, we should expect:

- To frequently say and do things to hurt each other's feelings since we're all imperfect
- This may occur even once (or more) every day or two
- It's perfectly normal, and should be expected
- That you'll have to learn how to address and heal these feelings so they don't build and harm the relationship

These emotional feelings run underneath conflict. This may run counter to your assumptions about what's "normal" for relationships. But it's reality—we just aren't prepared for it. Remember, we haven't learned how to talk about these negative feelings from sustained hurts that naturally occur in a relationship. We are deeply emotional human beings who can be easily slighted and hurt by those we love so deeply. The problem is that one cannot ignore these feelings. When suppressed too long internal pressure builds up. The feelings burst as anger rises to the surface and conflict begins, or repeats. This sucks vitality from a relationship, and over time can severely damage love feelings. Intensity of romantic love in a relationship fades in proportion to frequency of harmful conflict. The question is how can you prevent this from happening.

Principle #3:
Reduce Conflict With Softly Specific Co-Coaching

The solution is to respectfully share these negative feelings in such a way that successful healing occurs and conflict is reduced. This is the aim of the third principle, Softly Specific Co-Coaching, which is a process for open, honest communication to heal any negative feelings arising in a relationship. It's has a triple purpose:

1. Changing NRPs
2. Meeting love needs
3. Handling everyday conflict

Here you and your partner agree to take full responsibility for the happiness of your relationship. Each person takes ownership for changing his or her own NRPs, meeting each other's love needs, and addressing any disagreements respectfully. Importantly, you commit to giving helpful, constructive feedback when falling off track with those efforts. The goal is to achieve the most authentic, deeply loving connection possible.

What happens in most relationships is that couples make generalized complaints of frustration to one another about their needs and wants. Unfortunately these are not behaviorally specific enough. It's assumed this should be enough to spur change. When it doesn't, the conclusion is made that the partner can't or won't.

However, to change NRP behaviors it will require ongoing feedback from you and your partner. This is what's required for learning how to become proficient at any new behavior or skill. We all need helpful feedback—that's simply what it takes to change behavior. Each of us will easily become forgetful when trying to change behavior. In fact, it should be expected that we would fall off track without coaching feedback from a partner. Without co-coaching, it's almost impossible to have a relationship based on growth aimed at changing key behaviors and patterns of conflict.

Development of the Co-Coaching Process

What led to the idea of co-coaching? Actually, I first began using this co-coaching process in the business world to help develop more effective leadership teams. Leaders on a team are taught to give open, mutual, respectful feedback about personal development goal areas. The optimal result is a more open culture where everyone works better within the team. After seeing this work so well with management teams, I began to expand the idea of co-coaching to marriage counseling.

One of the biggest problems in making relationships work is that we're not taught the subtle social-relationship skills of how to effectively speak with one another when we have difficult issues to discuss. Because of this, so many conflicts occur in business, personal relationships, and especially in marriage. The normal response to annoying or upsetting behavior for most couples is to wait until the frustration builds up to the point where it can no longer be contained. Then, one reacts with some form of verbally aggressive behavior involving one or more of the first 14 NRPs, which begets more conflict.

How to nicely point out the negative behavior of a partner? Most people don't know how to do this. Yet it's one of the absolutely critical skills needed to help make a relationship successful. In Softly Specific Co-Coaching you learn the skill of how to respectfully communicate hurt feelings, needs, and give feedback to one another. This is invaluable for achieving long-term relationship happiness and success.

Nowhere in romantic love stories on TV, in movies, or in books, did any of us see or hear how to respectfully confront the love of our life with feedback regarding behaviors we don't like. No one told you before walking down the aisle in marriage that this would be one of the most important skills you could ever learn!

Cautionary Note

Before introducing the specific methods of Softly Specific Co-Coaching, however, a few things must be said about how you should or shouldn't use this process. For those having *significant* problems (harmful recurring conflict or severe loss of loving feelings), these techniques should be used with the help of a well-trained couples' therapist for two very good reasons.

First, your NRPs and corresponding emotional hurts will make it difficult, if not impossible, for you to try and do this independently. That's to be expected; it's no reflection on you or the "save-ability" of your relationship. Couples locked in repeating conflict have blind spots. It will be difficult for each of you to see your part objectively and non-defensively take ownership.

Second, the Softly Specific Co-Coaching method involves a form of communicating that is different from the common ways that most couples handle conflict. It requires repeated practice of new skills that are challenging to learn because of ingrained cultural conditioning using poor, ineffective methods. Attempting this process on your own and failing may make you both feel worse or even hopeless: *See, we've tried another thing and it didn't work, so this proves we're not meant for one another.* Be careful to avoid this, get the help you need. Consider this the warning you see regarding dangerous stunts or extreme sports—*don't try to do this on your own.* Use the knowledge gained here to help guide you in finding the right couples therapist.

The Heart of Co-Coaching: Authentic Communication

The term Softly Specific Co-Coaching is defined not only as a specific technique, but also as a larger philosophy of continued open communication aimed at mutual self-improvement and deeper love connection. It is the agreement to share one's deepest feelings and love needs, and to confront negative behaviors. Both partners take on this commitment for making the relationship successful.

This method for reducing conflict was developed after years of seeing couples having so much trouble in changing their relationship because they were locked into repeating patterns of conflict. This was personally frustrating until finally the following very important realization came to me: Most relationship conflict is caused by two behaviors, which if eliminated could prevent it from ever happening.

Two Primary Factors Trigger Conflict

Think about it: most conflict involves one of two very specific behaviors, which are high risk for escalating any discussion with your partner into conflict:

1. Aggressive voice tone or words
2. Generalized negative value judgments.

Both behaviors will almost always be perceived as a threat to one's self-esteem. The expression of any degree of aggressive voice tone or anger elicits a naturally occurring fight-or-flight defensive response. It causes an almost uncontrollable defensiveness for whoever is on the receiving end. The term "aggressive voice tone" is used here to help couples avoid the debate over whether overt anger versus covert anger is being expressed. Often disagreement occurs with one partner saying, "You're wrong! I'm not really angry; I'm just annoyed (or irritated, upset)."

It finally struck me after watching couple after couple for over 27 years of doing marital therapy that *any* form of even slightly elevated and irritated voice tone, frustration, or mild anger is perceived as a threating to self or self-esteem. When this happens, most couples are unable to stop from arguing. Conflict is rarely, if ever, resolved through expressing any type of anger, even subtler lower level expressions of it such as annoyance and irritation. In fact, it's usually a subtle accusatory or blaming voice tone of voice that most commonly kicks off a disagreement.

When explaining this to couples for the first time, I demonstrate by looking them straight in the eyes and saying something to them in a stern, moderately aggressive tone of voice. Then, I repeat back to them the same sentence, but in a completely neutral or pleasant voice tone. I ask what kind of physiological reaction they felt within their body in the first instance.

Clients always tell me the same thing: They experienced some degree of mild anxiousness, fear, or startled response. And remember, my demonstration with them involves using only a mildly aggressive voice tone, not raising my voice louder. This demonstration helps couples better understand the defensive reaction felt when there's any degree of aggressive, angry verbal expression.

Here's an important question for you to ask yourself right now: Have you ever had a conflict in your relationship where one or both of these behaviors have not been present?

Culture Promotes Sloppy Conflict Resolution

Unfortunately, cultural messaging reinforces the belief that it is important and even healthy to express anger. For example, there's the popular notion that a person shouldn't hold anger in or bottle it up—one must express it. This is even reinforced by some therapists. The problem is not that people need to express anger to be psychologically healthy. Rather, they do need to learn how to be more assertive in communicating in a nonaggressive way, which will be empowering—likely resulting in a positive outcome. This is the healthiest way to express oneself. And this is exactly what Softly Specific Co-Coaching is all about.

It is also typical for most people to utilize negative generalizations during a conflict, rather than being more behaviorally specific in a way that would avoid perceived threats to the other person's self-worth. Using a generalization that has any kind of negative connotation will also immediately cause an internal protective reaction in a partner to fight back.

It's a subconscious reaction to feelings of being affronted by his or her partner.

Once again, we have never been taught how to prevent conflict by avoiding these two behaviors. Let's break down these two behaviors further as illustrated just below:

Two Key Conflict-Creating Behaviors

1. Aggressive voice tone and words
   - Elevated, raised voice
   - Blaming, accusatory, or complaining voice tone and words
   - Irritability, impatience, annoyance, irritation, terseness
   - Overt anger

2. Generalized global negative value judgments
   - *You never think about me; you're selfish; you never help out*, and other generalizations

High Respect-Based Conflict Resolution

It requires reconditioning ourselves not to engage in the above two triggering behaviors. Instead, we need to learn how to communicate during potentially heated discussions with two *new* counteracting positive behaviors. These alternatives, listed below, will help de-escalate the situation, avoid conflict, and be more likely result in a positive outcome.

1) Be respectful in voice tone and word choice.
2) Point out specific behaviors without any generalizations or negative value judgments.

The Softly Specific Co-Coaching method is designed just for this reason. It helps train us in how to become skilled in these two positive behaviors for communicating. The entire Softly Specific process and its six steps center upon the elimination and control of these two core incendiary behaviors. The words *softly* and *specific* make it easy to remember the dual purpose.

This is not easy for any of us to learn and at first will seem unnatural or foreign since it's different from our usual way of handling conflict. Softly Specific is all about a very high level of respect and accountability. Possibly for the first time we are being asked to take total responsibility for being 100 percent respectful in the way we communicate with a romantic partner.

It's no longer okay to indulge in reacting with any expressions of anger or making lazy negative generalizations. Yes, if you think this might be a hard to do, you are right! It's the way all of us should have been taught to handle difficult discussions but we were never trained in the social etiquette for effectively resolving conflict. Instead, we've been reinforced in just the opposite way—how to escalate conflict!

So, while it will feel very unnatural at first and will require considerable practice, it's well worth it. I've found that couples that commit to using Softly Specific are often able to dramatically reduce repeating conflict patterns, change NRPs, and better meet each other's love needs. In fact, it's really quite amazing. Here is the easy-to-follow process. It utilizes some well-known, accepted best practices for couples communication combined with some additional creative twists and special-refinements.

Softly Specific Co-Coaching^{SM}

Part One: Offer Feedback and Request Behavior Change

1) **Identify vulnerable emotional feeling and specific negative behavior.**
   I feel _____ (non-angry vulnerable feelings: e.g. hurt, afraid, disappointed, disrespected, sad, rejected, unloved etc.) *when you do or say*
   _____
   (specifically describing the negative behavior to be changed).

2) **Make a request for specific behavior change.**
   Would you please instead do or say
   _____ ?
   (Specifically describing the positive behavior that's desired in the future)

3) **Make a request for ongoing commitment to changing future behavior.**
   Could you do this for me from now on?

Part Two: Partner Responds to Feedback and Behavior Change Request (this will be covered in detail in the following chapter)

4) **Clarify and paraphrase**
5) **Show empathy**
6) **Take ownership and sincerely apologize**

This is an exceedingly powerful communication technique. When couples learn to use this simple six-step process, they can learn to take control of repeating conflict. On occasion a client will say to me, "But this is just a technique. We have real, deeper, more important issues to discuss than just communication." Here's the problem: Deeper issues cannot be resolved until we first change the way we communicate to prevent difficult discussions from escalating into conflict. It's not about who is right or wrong in a disagreement, rather it's about how you both respectfully communicate differences and resolve them.

As noted earlier, when I first talk with couples they most commonly say their biggest problem is in "communication" that ends too often in conflict. What I've found is that these communication problems invariably stem from deeply ingrained habits of using the two key behaviors triggering conflict—verbal aggressiveness and generalizations. The Softly Specific is thus a communication technique that helps you take control of these two behaviors that normally trigger conflict. You learn how to more effectively resolve any issue, no matter how difficult it might be.

How Most Arguments Start

Let's say a wife says in an aggressive voice tone, "You always think about yourself. You're so selfish and never think about me when you come home at night and what I need. I always have to be the one who puts the kids to bed!" This is an accusatory, blaming generalization (NRP #11). It makes a global negative value judgment about the husband being selfish. We can all guess where this one is headed!

The husband might feel deeply offended that his wife is referring to him as selfish. He works hard as a provider throughout the day for his wife and family. He helps out in many other ways with home responsibilities. The perceived attack to his self-worth makes it difficult for him to respond in an open, non-defensive way. Does any of this sound familiar?

Softly, Powerfully Assertive

Let's see what might happen if the wife used the Softly Specific method using a nice tone of voice: "Honey, I feel so hurt and dismissed when you don't share more of the responsibility for putting the kids to bed at night. I've mentioned to you before that I really would like some help. Could please help me by putting the kids to bed every other night? Could you do that for me from now on?"

Notice that the wife has empowered herself by not using any aggressive tone or making any generalized accusations about her husband being selfish. Rather than being perceived as a nagging complainer, she directly asserts her need in the form of a specific request. She takes further legitimate power by asking for the ongoing commitment to change future behavior. By communicating in this way, her husband is much more likely to respond in a positive way. It's such a simple communication principle!

So many conflicts could be avoided in relationships if this were the standard socially acceptable way of handling disagreement. Maybe someday in the future it will become everyday conflict-resolving etiquette. In the meantime, you and I are faced with having to unlearn culturally ingrained bad habits and learn new, better ones.

In fact, Softly Specific, when used correctly, allows one to take control of all of the first fourteen NRP aggressive influencing and defense behaviors. In doing this, you can avoid giving a partner any justifiable reason to get upset or aggressive. Let's take a look at how Softly Specific might help you and your relationship by looking at an actual client situation.

Case Example:
I Don't Feel We Know How to Communicate

A good example of the power of learning to give feedback using Softly Specific is Amber and Chris, a couple married for ten years. Amber stated in the first telephone call, "I don't feel we know how to communicate," complaining they frequently bickered. Both tended to get easily angry and quickly reactive with each other in a way that was visible to others in their family. Both worked hard on the first three steps of delivering Softly Specific feedback trying to soften voice tone whenever they spoke to one another which substantially reduced conflict. In fact, Amber reported that her mother commented to her about the observed change in behavior after a few therapy sessions saying, "You guys are 50 percent better than the last time I saw you!"

By the ninth session both made such good progress that they were ready to stop counseling. At that time, Amber said that Chris had worked very hard on his number 1 NRP of not listening. And Chris said Amber worked very hard on her worst NRP of using an overly aggressive, elevated voice tone.

They had committed to changing these patterns and giving feedback to one another more softly. For example, Amber said when Chris starts to fall back into his old pattern, she'll say, "Honey, you're not paying enough attention to what I'm saying right now." And when Amber slips into her pattern of starting to get angry, he'll say to her, "Honey, it seems like you're starting to feel a little excited and your voice is elevating."

In the last session both said that there had been a remarkable change in their frequent arguments, which they estimated had been occurring once or twice a day before coming in for therapy. Now, they have an argument only about once a week and immediately begin using Softly Specific, which helps avoid any serious arguments. Chris said that using Softly Specific feedback allowed them to "stop things that in the past would normally have blown into something you can't imagine!"

Reducing conflict helped free them up to meeting identified love needs. It has restored their relationship, and strengthened their emotional connection to a very high level of marital happiness and gratification.

Gentleness and Kindness Make a Happy Marriage

Gottman's research on long-term relationship success further supports the idea of "softening" in teaching couples how to handle conflict. He says a "harsh startup," marked by criticism, sarcasm, or a form of contempt usually results in a very poor outcome for discussions:

> Statistics tell the story: 96% of the time you can predict the outcome of the conversation based on the first three minutes of the 15-minute interaction! A harsh start up simply dooms you to failure.[12]

In happy marriages the initiating partner, usually the wife, softens the discussion by starting off using soothing methods of de-escalation, and her partner responds favorably. Gottman concluded his research points to a "gentleness model of marital therapy" and says:

> Marriages that are working well are characterized by a specific form of gentleness and kindness toward one another that involves starting a discussion of a marital issue in a softened way and accepting influence from one another.[13]

In general, his research shows that the more aggressive arguments are, the more potentially damaging to the relationship. He found not only that a harsh start-up is harmful but that sustained negativity in the form of four specific types of interaction is particularly lethal to a relationship: criticism, contempt, defensiveness, and stonewalling.[14]

Hence, there is overwhelming scientific research support for not only softening, but also for the overall modulating and reducing of aggressiveness in relationships for their success. Softly Specific was designed to be a simply structured, highly disciplined method to eliminate both harsh start-up and any aggressive behaviors escalating conflict. In fact, its first two steps parallel some of Gottman's recommendations for "softened startup."[15]

Actually, softening is the best approach to use in handling conflict with any person in any situation. Some of my clients have used variations of Softly Specific for dealing with children or work situations. However, there are important modifications to be made in those situations beyond the scope of this book (see www.relationshipcocoaching .com).

Softening By Expressing Vulnerable Emotions

Asking couples to talk about vulnerable feelings—being hurt, sad, scared—with Softly Specific rather than anger is designed to serve as a natural softening agent. Other leaders in research on marriage support the importance of softening through expressing vulnerable feelings instead of anger. Dr. Andrew Christensen and Dr. Neil Jacobson's *Integrated Couples Therapy* has shown a 75 percent recovery rate for couples and it emphasizes softening for couples by encouraging them to use "soft disclosures" of vulnerable feelings rather than "hard disclosures" of angry, accusatory expressions to reduce conflict and promote empathetic acceptance.[16]

In addition, Dr. Susan Johnson's research on Emotionally Focused Couples Therapy, which has also shown a high therapeutic improvement rate, demonstrates the importance of dealing with deeper emotionally vulnerable feelings. She refers to "softening" when a partner expresses underlying emotions taking a "softer, more vulnerable stance."[17]

It seems the skill of learning to express vulnerable emotions and empathetically receive them is absolutely important for achieving relationship success. Once again, we ask ourselves: Why isn't this something we are all taught to do?

Most people have difficulty getting in touch with and verbalizing vulnerable feeling states; surface feelings of anger are more comfortable, providing a feeling of power and protection. But most serious relationship conflict usually stems from deeper vulnerable feelings such as hurt, rejection, and fears of abandonment. This is where one must learn to *downshift* from the anger and surface complaints to the deeper level of emotional awareness.

One of the primary purposes of Softly Specific is to help you gain control of and change harmful conflict to support you in feeling safer and more secure in sharing these deeper vulnerable feelings. The problem is that emotional wounds become encrusted with an outer layer of habitual defensive anger supported by protective NRPs and cyclical conflict. This makes it sometimes very tough for us to break through to a deeper emotionally vulnerable level.

Using Softly Specific to *Downshift*

One of the most important ways to help you emotionally downshift is the instruction in Step One for Softly Specific. One partner is asked to always start out by expressing the underlying vulnerable feelings, not the protective surface feelings of anger, which cause more conflict. This immediately sets a softer tone for the conversation being more likely to lead to a positive outcome.

"I feel" statements have been a long-standing recommended technique for couples when communicating in some marital therapy circles. In fact, as a marriage therapist, I used to do this all the time with couples. But it never seemed to help reduce conflict. Then I realized the problem: If you ask couples to make therapeutic "I feel" messages with no restrictions, they tend to express anger more often. It's less likely they will take the time to identify and share deeper, vulnerable feelings underneath that anger.

Using unrestricted "I feel" statements can give tacit approval for anger. It gives therapeutic license for partners to avoid going deeper in awareness, below surface feelings of anger. And it offers unspoken permission for couples in counseling to continue sharing angry feelings in an aggressive way.

Consequently, Step One of the Softly Specific prohibits the expression of any anger or aggressive voice tone and requires you to start off any difficult conversation by sharing the vulnerable feeling underneath any anger. In therapy, I've found this helps facilitate couples getting more quickly to deeper emotional levels.

For example, in a session with a highly analytical husband who rarely shows any emotions, we explored his feeling of being "shut down." He reported feeling numb with no feelings of any kind for his wife for the past three weeks after she made an angry, hurtful statement that they might be divorced in five years.

It's important to point out, this client prided himself on the fact that he was very logical, objective, and rarely showed emotions. I asked him to use the Softly Specific to downshift from the feeling of being shut down to the vulnerable feelings underneath. Suddenly, his eyes became red and he began to tear-up saying: "I felt like my umbilical cord was ripped out." He went on to describe how he felt she was breaking her commitment making him feel deeply hurt and scared. We explored the obvious attachment issues in his relationship with a mother who was never there for him during childhood. He and siblings had to totally fend for themselves. The way he handled the pain of his mother's absence was to "shut down" his emotional feelings in the same way and "prove I could take care of myself, no matter what happened."

His wife said that she had never seen her husband share feelings at such a level of vulnerability. She let down her defenses immediately, began to cry, and became exceptionally compassionate and reassuring. It was a therapeutic breakthrough for this couple!

Focusing on Specific Behavior Avoids Conflict

The other component to Step One of Softly Specific is that you need to objectively define specific behavior. Refraining from generalized negative value judgments that are threating to self-worth is equally essential.

Resentment toward partners is typically reinforced through generalized negative value judgments supporting what I refer to as core emotional grievances. These refer to generalized beliefs that serve to kindle relationship conflict, such as *You're emotionally distant; never think of me; always take advantage of me; never listen to my opinion.*

As soon as our partner lets us down in some way, we tend to take that incident and file it away in memory as further data that proves our generalized emotional grievance is indeed true. And, of course, since angry, aggressive feelings provide us with a greater sense of personal power and protection than hurt feelings, we tend to instantaneously *upshift* from hurt to powerful feelings of anger that make the situation worse.

However, when expressing concerns to partners, if there's no threat to one's self-esteem caused by global negative value statements, then there's nothing to react defensively about. This is a powerful form of empowered, yet very respectful-assertiveness; there's just a request for specific behavior to be changed. When you make Step One a fundamental guideline for all communication, big change can begin to occur in conflict patterns!

Healing *Core Emotional Grievances*

Using Softly Specific also helps heal core emotional grievances relating to ongoing frustrations resulting from unmet love needs and NRPs. It's here where partners feel the most unloved. While reducing conflict one can more closely examine the accuracy of global negative assumptions you've made about one another. Do you know what the core emotional grievances are in your relationship? Where do you feel the most hurt or angry?

By using Softly Specific you can determine the kernel of truth versus mistaken assumptions made in the generalizations of your core grievances. Deep healing can occur exactly at this point as partners come to the awareness of how they are causing emotional hurt and then can make commitments to change behavior. Overall, Softly Specific is a training in the art of subtle social-relationship skills to be more thoughtful, sensitive, and accurate in how to talk about potentially difficult issues to prevent the buildup of hurt feelings. Take some time now and explore in the exercises that follow how to apply this principle to your relationship and reduce unnecessary conflict.

Self-Exploration Exercises

1) Take time to examine your relationship and how conflict is triggered by your use of aggressive voice tone and words and generalized negative value judgments.
2) Consider how you might utilize these first three Softly Specific steps when you approach your partner to talk about anything with potential for conflict.
3) Repeatedly practice each of the first three steps of the Softly Specific with your partner, starting with potentially less heated situations. As you become more skilled, begin to apply it in everyday situations that have potential for conflict.

(Note: Remember, if you have serious problems in your relationship, you should enlist the help of an experienced marital therapist.)

Our focus up to this point has been primarily on how to deliver feedback and share feelings with one's partner. The next chapter will present details regarding how the receiver of feedback can best respond and how to use Softly Specific in day-to-day situations to reduce conflict in your relationship.

The Relationship Co-Coaching Model for Dynamic Growth

1. Fulfill Partner's Love Needs
2. Identify and Change Negative Relationship Patterns (NRPs)
3. Reduce Conflict with Softly Specific Co-Coaching
4. Seek Relationship Self-Actualization and Altruistic Love

Chapter 5

Receive Co-Coaching Feedback: Stop Repeating Conflict

In a love relationship, where you bare your soul at the deepest emotional level, it's hard to continue opening up to someone who has injured your feelings but stubbornly refuses to simply say they're sorry.

Now that you've learned how to deliver feedback to a partner in a non-aggressive way, it's also important to learn how to be on the receiving end of feedback. Defensiveness escalates conflict further, yet it's one of the biggest problems I see with couples—they simply don't know how to sincerely take ownership. This leaves each partner not feeling heard or understood, the result being no resolution.

How often does this happen in your relationship? How well do you and your partner listen, refrain from defensiveness, and sincerely apologize. If you're like most of us, you probably are not very good at this so let's go to the next skill to learn—how to graciously and non-defensively listen to your partner's feelings, needs, requests, and show empathetic caring; without this it will be difficult, if not impossible, to learn how to resolve issues without residual negative feelings later resurfacing.

Softly Specific Co-Coaching for Receiver

Here are the three Softly Specific steps for receiving feedback:

1. **Clarify and paraphrase**
    - *Could you clarify further, be more specific, or give me some examples?* (Skip this step if partner has been totally clear and specific)
    - Wait for response.

2. **Show empathy**
    - *I can totally understand (or appreciate, etc.) why you would feel_____ when I _____* (describe specific behavior).
    - Also affectionately touch partner in caring way (if it's OK with him or her).

3. **Take ownership and sincerely apologize**
    - *I apologize; I'm sorry and I will_____* (describe new positive behavior).
    In this case, in a non-defensive way, you look for that aspect of your partner's feedback about your behavior that has real validity—the kernel of truth to it; you take full ownership for it. This apology should be free of any justifications or "explanations," such as: *I'm sorry for hurting your feelings, but I only did this because you did (or said) what you did; it wasn't my intention to hurt you, etc.*

Clarify Feedback

Each of these steps is very important, especially Step #1 of clarification. Quite often the one delivering feedback is not fully clear regarding specific behaviors and may fall back into making a negative generalization. If this happens, avoid becoming defensive or aggressive. Rather, help your partner identify the specific behaviors he or she wants changed.

Doing this is actually very empowering, removing you from being the victim of blaming and complaining from any global attacks on self-worth by your partner. This is actually far more effective as a protective defense than anger or NRPs. However, it does necessitate developing a genuine interest in learning how you might better meet the needs of your partner.

Empathy

Step #2 of showing empathy is very important. Asking partners to share deeper feelings regarding how love needs are not being met offers an opportunity to take emotional engagement to a new level. Showing empathy and understanding and validating the feelings of your partner are extraordinarily healing.

The relationship skill of showing empathy is generally not taught, especially to men. In our society males often are culturally reinforced for being more analytical and not feeling-oriented. It's quite common that women's love needs for being listened to, appreciated, and understood are unmet due to the man's failure to show empathy. As a result, I do a great deal of empathy training with husbands.

The skill of empathy involves three parts. First, one demonstrates a sincere interest in listening to the feelings of the partner. This means being fully emotionally present in eye contact, body language, and other nonverbal communication. Second, it's not trying to "fix the problem" and instead asking occasional questions to promote further in-depth discussion. Third, and most important, it involves making occasional empathetic statements, such as, *I'm so sorry that's happening; that's tough*; or *I can totally understand why you would feel that way*. The latter statement, of course, is exactly what's used for step two. You'll find that hearing this from your partner in a sincere way has an extraordinarily positive healing effect.

Ownership and Apology

Step #3, taking ownership and making a sincere apology is one of the most incredibly powerful love skills that a person can learn. There's nothing more frustrating than someone who won't apologize, or does so with justifications. How good are you and your partner at non-defensively apologizing?

Taking responsibility and sincerely apologizing is difficult for many people. Too often when one does apologize, the tendency is to give justifications for it: *I'm sorry for getting so angry with you,* **but** *you made me do it when you did or said XYZ*. Again, perhaps it's human nature to feel the need to justify and protect oneself. This is certainly another instance where there is little social modeling, and yet this is such a powerful skill!

When I ask couples to practice these three steps, it's really amazing to see the effect on the partners receiving the apology. There's an emotional and physical relaxation in clients' faces and bodies when finally getting the apology they've wanted for so long.

I've found that Softly Specific greatly speeds the healing of hurt feelings to help establish a deeper, more meaningful love connection. And the completely non-defensive, sincere apology is the key to this healing. In one couple's session, a wife complained that her husband had *never* apologized to her in the course of their marriage. After I gently challenged him and showed the proper steps for taking ownership and apologizing with Softly Specific, he gave her his first real, non-justified apology. It was wonderful to see her reaction of immense emotional relief. She had finally been validated, a real breakthrough for the couple.

The Justification Apology: *You Made Me Act That Way*

An apology seems like such a simple thing. However in relationships there's one barrier that gets in the way. Partners often have a hard time apologizing because they feel that it was the other one who "started it" by doing or saying something that caused them to get upset.

They have a feeling of righteousness: *I would never have done this or said that if my partner hadn't done or said XYZ. I ordinarily would never have reacted that way.* I hear clients say this all the time. What clouds the situation further is that in many situations it's also difficult to determine who really *was* the first person to become aggressive or engage in NRPs. Both may have very quickly become aggressive.

This is one of the most common dynamics seen in counseling. Couples try to present evidence as to why it was the other partner who caused trouble or made them react in the negative way they did. The one being accused is busy seeking release from culpability.

This feeling of defensive justification runs very deep in each partner. Even if the therapist temporarily stops the defensiveness by pointing out that it really doesn't matter who started the conflict, the accused partner is most likely to continue feeling justified, secretly feeling that the other person is the real problem. My bet is that you can relate to this feeling of defensive justification; we've all had it during conflicts. In my opinion it's a central underlying dynamic that supports conflict and makes it so difficult for partners to reach resolution. The one behavior that helps end any conflict is really quite simple. It's the act of one person simply owning negative behavior and sincerely apologizing.

After many years of working with couples, I had seen this defensive justification pattern play out over and over again until several years ago a solution intuitively came to me as a remedy for conflict in my own marriage. I had become aware of this mutual blame pattern as an underlying cause for much of the repeating conflict in my own marriage—my wife and I *both* believed it was the other who first started it! One day after a disagreement, the solution came to me in a flash.

The No-Excuses Agreement for *Any* Verbal Aggression

The only way to stop this blaming pattern is that both partners must make a no-excuse agreement for any verbally aggressive behavior. The agreed-upon principle here is that it doesn't matter who starts the aggressive behavior—or NRP—you both make the agreement that there is no excuse under any circumstances for becoming verbally aggressive or falling back into NRPs. One can *always* find a reason for becoming aggressive so there must be a pact that there is never any excuse for it. This is an approach of high accountability. Partners are 100 percent responsible for controlling their own verbally aggressive behavior—including all of the first 14 NRPs. From a logical standpoint, it just makes sense. There's no other way to stop the endless defensive justification between partners. Anything less than this invites a courtroom-like debate over who really started it.

When my wife and I made this agreement, it helped us immeasurably in reducing disagreements. Within a short time, I began using it with couples and found that it was incredibly effective for helping them in breaking blame patterns. It halts the blame game within the therapy session, and more importantly it helps prevent or reduce the intensity of conflict at home if couples continue to hold each other responsible for this agreement.

I've never seen anything more effective in putting a stop to partners making excuses for becoming aggressive. It's not someone else causing them to act in an aggressive way; it's choosing to respond aggressively rather than in a more constructive manner. This establishes a new belief system calling for accountability regarding aggressive verbal behavior.

This no-excuse agreement is central to making the Softly Specific process work. Without it, the partner receiving the feedback inevitably reacts by saying, "But I can't apologize because I really feel that my partner made me act this way." And then the whole process stops dead. So, this agreement is essential.

When couples commit to using the Softly Specific process with the no-excuses agreement, and choose to have a relationship based upon co-coaching, meeting love needs, and changing NRPs, then, wow, this greatly improves the chances that they'll be able to move forward. Let's look at an example of a couple that made this commitment to co-coaching with Softly Specific and how conflict in their relationship drastically changed.

Case Example:
We Can't Get Engaged Because We Fight Too Much

This client situation is a good example of how couples develop repeating patterns of destructive arguments. A young couple came for counseling. Steve was in his mid-thirties, and Joan in her late twenties. They had been together for just one-and-a-half years. Both were considering becoming engaged, but had such frequent arguments—several times a week—they felt it unwise to take that next step. In the first session, both of them admitted to getting easily hurt which then escalated to anger. In fact they acknowledged that they both had trouble seeing the other person's position.

They described their relationship as being very good most of the time with a lot of positive aspects, but just that they easily became argumentative over relatively small issues. In fact, Joan said, "Sometimes we are mad just because we want to be mad." And Steve added, "We may get a rush from anger or there may be a certain threshold of anger and we may need it."

Both acknowledged that the majority of the first 14 NRPs were a problem for each one of them in their arguments. Unfortunately, part of the pattern was that Joan would become so hurt in the process of fighting that she'd often break up with him. She'd left Steve a number of times in the past after arguments.

The couple learned the Softly Specific process in the very first session to help them break this cycle of arguments. Both admitted that their biggest problem was defensiveness. Each had extreme difficulty in being open to hearing feedback from each other if it was at all critical. So learning how to accept and receive feedback with Softly Specific was particularly important for this couple.

Within just a few sessions, both reported they had totally stopped having any arguments after the very first session when they used Softly Specific at home. Although we did do some work in identifying love needs, both said that for the most part they were already fulfilling those needs for each other. The only real problem was this seriously harmful pattern of arguments, which reinforced further hurt feelings and stubborn defensiveness.

After just four or five sessions, it was obvious their depth of love and connection had changed. Both were much more loving and affectionate with one another. They looked like two love birds wrapped around each other as they sat on the sofa in the waiting room.

And after the fifth session, Steve and Joan reported they had not experienced any arguments or fights since after the first session when they began using Softly Specific at home. They had mastered the process so well that they were ready to stop counseling and were now seriously considering getting engaged. This is an excellent example of how committing to an open, honest co-coaching relationship and using Softly Specific helped a couple learn how to break free of their NRPs in a very short period of time.

But I Know I'm Right and You're Wrong!

There's one other important classic conflict situation that needs to be discussed. In any relationship you'll on occasion experience a stalemate. This usually starts by both of you having a disagreement in recalling an incident or having a difference of opinion. Each of you insists that you are correct regarding the details of what you're arguing about, sure that your partner is wrong. A back-and-forth ensues with things getting heated. You each have a hard time giving up the argument because, of course, you know that you're right!

Does this sound familiar? I'm sure it does. It seems to be human nature that the capacity for each of us to *know* that we're right far exceeds the ability to acknowledge that we might be wrong. So here's the incredibly simple solution that many of you may have heard before—just agree to disagree! Here's how it works: When you get in the middle of one of these memory recall impasses, just say:

> You and I have very different memories of what happened. You think you're right and I think I'm right. Neither of us will ever convince the other that we're wrong, so let's just agree to disagree. There'll be times in our relationship in which we agree to disagree, that's expected and it's okay. So let's not argue any further about it and move forward.

This is actually very empowering. You may find yourself getting very irritated with a partner who continues to insist he or she is right and you're wrong. It's a great way to immediately stop this in a very respectful, logically irrefutable way.

Assumptions of Negative Intent

As can easily happen in a relationship, you may drop the ball or do something to hurt your partner's feelings. However, they may make an incorrect assumption about the intention behind your behavior. In this case, you still need to first own the specific negative behavior, and then later correct the assumptions. Be careful that you're not just being defensive and trying to justify your actions. Your sole motivation here is that you're trying to help your partner feel more emotionally secure.

For example, one partner says, "When you didn't call me last night while on your trip, I felt that you really didn't love me." The other partner might then say, "I can appreciate you feeling hurt that way when I didn't call as I'd promised. I apologize for that; there's no excuse."

Pause for at least 60 seconds to avoid sounding defensive. Then say,

"I do want you to know that doesn't mean I don't love you, since I love you more than anything. Our business meeting lasted much later than expected and when I got back to the hotel room it was so late I was afraid to call and wake you. I didn't know you'd want me to call even if it's late, so I'll be sure to do that in the future."

For the person delivering the feedback, it's also very important to watch out when making assumptions and learn to first check them out, such as saying, "I'm assuming that you said or did this because of xyz. Is that correct?" Couples who learn this skill to check out the validity of their assumptions quickly discover that those assumptions, often of negative intention, are frequently incorrect.

Co-Coaching Feedback for Slip-ups

One important clarification: The measure of success in using Co-Coaching and Softly Specific should not necessarily be based on the total elimination of all conflict. That's because we're all imperfect. With the daily stresses in life, it's easy to fall back into behaviors such as using an aggressive voice tone, making generalizations, or NRPs. For example, in busy times, it's natural on occasion to act irritated, impatient, and terse (NRP #10) with a partner. It happens to all of us. Each of us at some point will hurt our partner's feelings and return to NRPs. The goal is a major reduction in frequency of conflict. However, another equally important measure of success is that slip-ups are handled with co-coaching feedback in a relatively smooth, positive way. When we sometimes fail at de-escalating conflict, as we all will do, the post-conflict healing is also extremely important. Softly Specific is meant not only to reduce harshness and high levels of aggression that escalate conflict, it also aids in the healing work after an argument does occur. There's no better way to repair hurt feelings than partners showing empathy, taking ownership, and giving a no-excuse apology.

Violations of Softly Specific

There are two behaviors in that you'll need to be on the lookout for in order to keep conflict from recurring. As mentioned previously, these are the two instigating components contributing to most conflict—aggressive voice tone/words and generalizations. This is where slipups are most likely to occur, so whenever there are violations in step one, you should give coaching feedback by saying:

1) Can you please talk to me nicely right now; your voice tone is_____ (elevated, raised, terse, harsh, etc.).
2) Can you please make a specific request right now of what you want changed.

By remembering to coach one another regarding these two specific behaviors, you can begin to take control of conflict in your relationship. The foundation of the Co-Coaching relationship is to make the agreement to be fully responsible and remind each other to continually return to delivering Softly Specific feedback. It's a commitment to *always* talk to one another in a nice, respectful way!

Feedback Regarding Aggressive Voice Tone and Words

A common argument in relationships over disputed voice tone is that one partner tries to give feedback to the other that he or she "yells" too much. But the partner receiving the feedback defensively rejects it, saying, "I haven't been yelling." In his or her mind, there hasn't been any yelling. In these cases the defensive partner needs to receive more specific behavioral feedback as to subtle elevations in voice volume or tone that sounds harsh or terse.

In many conflicts there may not really be much elevation of voice but only a subtly blaming or accusatory aggressive tone or words perceived as snide, sarcastic, biting, etc. These little verbal barbs are very offensive and can easily start off an argument. When your partner does this, here's how to give feedback in a respectful, behaviorally specific way:

1. I feel hurt (or disrespected, sad, etc.) when your voice tone is aggressive (or elevated, accusatory, blaming, irritable, snide, sarcastic, etc.)
2. Instead would you please change your tone and talk to me nicely right now, no matter what we're discussing?
3. Could you do this for me?

This makes it easier for your partner to see how the communication has been disrespectful and take ownership. Since he or she has agreed to the no-excuses agreement, it leaves no room for argument.

Here's another personal story that may provide a good illustration of co-coaching feedback: Just this morning I was relaxing and taking some time for myself. I was thinking about what I would write in the next chapter of this book. My wife, who works in my counseling practice on administrative and billing issues, came in to discuss a business problem. She was pressed for time and needed a quick answer. Feeling irritated about the intrusion in my relaxing time, I responded back in a terse way with her, and I could immediately tell she didn't like it. Because we're both committed to Softly Specific, I gave her a genuine apology, which she accepted with no further negative feelings.

Without the simple healing balm of sincere apology, it's these repeated experiences of disrespectful voice tone over time that breed distance and blunting of romantic feeling in any relationship.

Feedback Regarding Generalized Criticisms

In addition to feedback about aggressive voice tone, it's equally important to ask your partner to stop making generalized criticisms and instead make a specific behavior request regarding what behavior she or he would like changed. This helps stop any outpouring of complaints, which would ordinarily cause you to feel overly criticized, harangued, or nagged.

Halting the global criticism helps couples in two ways: First, the person receiving this feedback can feel empowered by limiting any perceived attack, and second, the partner giving the feedback is more likely to get the request met because the perception of attack is avoided by being specific.

Quite simply, learning how to co-coach one another in these two behaviors of speaking nicely and making specific requests will help interrupt repetitive conflict that can quash deeper feelings of romantic love. Sustaining wonderful, romantic feelings throughout the stresses of life requires considerable nurturing and support. At the deepest level of feelings of love for our partner, we all tend to be sensitive to any aggressiveness in voice tone or accusatory generalizations, perceiving these as potential attacks to our esteem.

Everyone focuses upon the external gifts of romance like flowers or cards, but the greatest gift of love we can give each other is the everyday deep nurturing respect of always trying to speak nicely and being more thoughtful by not making generalized accusations. These are love skills that take motivation and practice. Nevertheless, these may be the most important gifts that you can give to keep the experience of deep love strong in your relationship.

Acceptance of Your Partner's Flaws

One point needs to be made about the whole process of Softly Specific. Although our goal is change in behavior, there must also be an understanding and acceptance of our imperfections. Changing long-standing patterns takes time.

I've found that couples naturally become more accepting of each other's imperfections when they see progress in better meeting one another's needs. The change doesn't have to be necessarily total, nor perfect. There's something healing and validating about a partner really listening to you and making a sincere effort to fulfill your needs to be loved. It tends to make all the difference in the world.

Loving your partner for everything, including flaws, is an ideal. But this becomes much easier when you see him or her working on improving areas of greatest importance to you. You'll never find a partner who is perfect, but you may find a partner who has many of the characteristics you want. And if he or she has a real desire to work on improving the relationship, then that kind of open, motivated person may be a partner *perfect for you*!

The importance of integrating change and acceptance is recognized in the research of Dr. Neil Jacobson and Dr. Andrew Christensen in Integrative Couple Therapy earlier mentioned. They found that interventions of acceptance as well as change show a more positive outcome compared to therapy without this dual focus. Emphasis upon acceptance helps generate tolerance and actually facilitates change because couples learn to be less affected by negative behaviors.[18]

Day-To-Day Conflict of Competing Needs

There are times in your relationship when there are competing needs, which don't necessarily involve deeper love needs or NRPs. One of you wants one thing and the other prefers something entirely different. For example, let's say one partner wants to spend a Saturday afternoon on the couch watching the game and the other wants to go to the art museum. In the normal day-to-day experience of a relationship, there will be competing needs such as this that often can escalate into a conflict if not handled properly.

What I've found in working with couples is they need to learn an important skill: brainstorming for a solution. Many couples tend to stop the discussion regarding competing needs after finding they're not in agreement. They fail to carry the conversation further, exploring how they might creatively meet both of their needs.

For example, consider the case of watching the game versus going to the art museum. The couple could have taken the discussion further to explore how they might accomplish both activities in one afternoon, or do one today and the other the next weekend. Couples too often feel frustrated when their desires are initially opposed and shut down the communication process way too early. So when discussing competing needs, make sure that you both stay in the discussion together and look for creative solutions!

Not a Quick Fix?

Let's pause here for a moment. You're learning new skills for deepening love in your relationship through Softly Specific Co-coaching. When you first picked up this book, you may have had certain expectations for what might be required of you to improve your relationship. When first coming in for couples counseling, clients may have a desire to find an expert who will *fix* their problems. However, creating real behavior change in a relationship takes work.

Softly Specific Practice Makes Perfect

In the beginning stages of counseling sessions many couples make the mistake of waiting until they have a heated argument before trying to practice

Softly Specific. This usually meets with failure since they haven't really embedded the new skills enough to change their usual NRPs when dealing with tough issues. So practice is paramount.

I've found that the best way for couples to learn Softly Specific is to give them the homework of practicing it a minimum of several times a week for at least six to eight weeks. It will feel awkward, even artificial at first. This is to be expected in learning any new skill. It won't necessarily feel genuine or sincere when one first starts practicing.

However it becomes smoother, feeling more natural after the new skill gradually develops. And when this happens, a breakthrough often occurs in the way couples handle conflict. It may take some couples just a few sessions while others might need ten to twenty therapy sessions, or more, before they become skilled. Some couples take longer because they're slow to practice the skill at home. Also, deeply habituated patterns of anger and NRPs may simply be hard to give up.

Some couples are not good at practicing the six steps of Softly Specific but follow the general principles of being softer and more specific in talking with one another. Subsequently, they generally see an initial marked improvement in lessening conflict, but it still can be easy to fall back into harmful patterns. Those couples that practice and follow each of the six steps carefully in a more disciplined way are more likely to see bigger reductions in conflict over time.

I frequently ask couples to debrief conflict that occurred since the last therapy session and redo it using Softly Specific. This helps them see how easy it would have been to resolve the conflict by correctly using Softly Specific. This kind of counseling requires a more therapeutic coaching approach to make sure a couple learns the Softly Specific steps (therapists, refer to Appendix B for details in being a "Marriage Therapist and Coach." and how this approach parallels the common principles of successful couples therapy proposed in a recent broad-based review of outcome research).

Putting the work into learning and then using the Softly Specific can have tremendous impact in your life; it's done so for my own marriage and I also see clients change in remarkable ways when they take the time to practice the six steps. In fact, it might be helpful to share some additional comments made to me just this past week by clients.

Ending Unstoppable Conflict Revitalizes Love

One couple made some interesting remarks worth sharing. They'd been married for 20 years, have two children, and in their first session complained about high levels of marital distress from daily arguments. In the past, they had tried everything to stop fighting, with no success, which left them feeling hopeless. Since beginning therapy, they had been working very hard in applying Softly Specific and making great progress. In our sixth session, the wife spontaneously made the following comment:

> I really like Softly Specific. We're both helping each other. It feels like a really positive thing for me to know I have an avenue to say what's on my mind. I'm really excited about it and I use it a lot.

Her husband joined in, saying:

> It's very natural. I know I have to practice in order to change something that's ingrained in me. There are ups and downs but it's a curve going upwards in our efforts to change. And so I know we may fumble and need to repeatedly pull the tools out.

I asked them if they could make a ballpark, subjective estimate regarding change in conflict. The couple said that by using Softly Specific they had reduced daily arguments from approximately fifteen mild to moderate conflicts a week to only two per week. And they estimated going from approximately five severe conflicts per month to none. Interestingly, the husband went on to say that he had actually used it with both of the children, ages eleven and fourteen, and found it very effective!

In conversation with a different couple, the wife shared how major reduction in conflict using Softly Specific affected feelings about her husband. She turned to him and said: *I'm really happy when you come home now. I'm so glad, so very grateful, rather than getting a nervous feeling and a lump in my throat out of fear when hearing the garage door open.*

These additional comments are given to offer hope for couples caught in continual cycles of conflict that seem unstoppable. It *is* possible to take control and break the chain of repetitive conflict to liberate and restore feelings of romance and fondness!

Softly Specific—"It's Like an App—a Software Platform"

In one session with a couple, the husband, who works in the information technology industry, made the following observation in describing the huge progress made in reducing conflicts since using the Softly Specific:

> It's like an app, a software platform that makes the task easier, in this case communication. And it changes the whole relationship. You're going to give someone a criticism, but you're making people check their weapons at the door and talk about it in a more civilized manner. It's helped us lay back our defensiveness and be more comfortable in talking about things. And we were at death's door since it was the third time we had discussed divorce so the overall change is really big.

Healing Deep Emotional Hurts

There are some situations where one or both partners have carried emotional hurt for many years marked by emotional distance, even estrangement. One wife at the start of counseling felt such emotional pain over her husband's failure to show any physical affection, sexual interest, or feelings of love for more than eight to ten years, she was ready to leave. However, after a number of sessions, he began to show demonstrable change in his behavior.

Even so, she expressed inability to get over the years of feeling abandoned. She complained that although she had expressed her feelings to him many times, she never felt truly heard or understood. I observed the reason for this was she was sharing feelings of anger rather than vulnerable feelings and he was apologizing defensively giving explanations of why he didn't mean to hurt her.

So both were coached in how to more carefully follow the Softly Specific: she showed more vulnerable feelings and he more empathy with complete ownership. Afterwards, she said it was the first time in years she felt fully understood and able to let go of her negative feelings. This shows how the Softly Specific offers a powerful way for couples to help heal long-standing, deeply rooted feelings.

Backsliding—It Happens to the Best!

Co-Coaching may be the most important of all the four principles. In fact, what I've found is that there are some couples that practice the Softly Specific steps and make major improvement. Over time though, they may fall back into old patterns of conflict if they stop the practice. One couple made such remarkable progress in just five months after conscientiously practicing Softly Specific they felt ready to stop therapy. They had even entered the six steps into their smartphones so they could use them no matter where they might be.

Yet, they returned to therapy four months later for a booster session after returning to old patterns of conflict. Both readily admitted the problem was that they had simply stopped using Softly Specific. After one booster session, they began diligently practicing Softly Specific once again and six weeks later reported by telephone that they had greatly reduced conflict and were back on track. This demonstrates the impact Softly Specific can have!

It's relevant to note there is interest in the field of marriage therapy in researching the effectiveness of follow-up sessions a year or two after therapy ends to help couples maintain long-term success. I always offer the option of booster sessions to all clients and urge them to call back anytime they might find themselves falling back to old patterns.

Co-Coaching: Long-Term Relationship Protection

So remember, when living with someone over many years there will be numerous times that you'll be unhappy with your partner's behavior; you'll both experience injured feelings. If you don't have a way to communicate those feelings, then resentment can build up, potentially harming the relationship. The Co-Coaching approach is to be used over the lifetime of a relationship. It's meant to help you and your partner nurture and sustain deep love through the ups and downs of life.

Self-Exploration Exercises

1) Take some time to think about how you and your partner receive feedback from one another. How well do you show empathy, apologize without justification? Identify where you both might improve by using Softly Specific.
2) Practice using each of the Softly Specific three steps for receiving feedback. (Once again, if there are serious issues in your relationship, work with a marital therapist before trying to use Softly Specific on your own.)
3) Discuss and role-play how you would both give each other feedback for slipups when using any aggressive voice tone or generalizations.
4) Brainstorm for creative solutions when you each have competing needs.

Learning Softly Specific is one of the most important skills for achieving a long-lasting, wonderful relationship. However, there is still a deeper belief change that must take place for you to ensure success in using the first three principles. The next chapter discusses this important shift in thinking.

The Relationship Co-Coaching Model for Dynamic Growth

1. Fulfill Partner's Love Needs
2. Identify and Change Negative Relationship Patterns (NRPs)
3. Reduce Conflict with Softly Specific Co-Coaching
4. Seek Relationship Self-Actualization and Altruistic Love

Chapter 6

A New Concept of Love for the 21st Century: Altruistic Love and Relationship Self-Actualization

It is important to consider the possibility that cultural programming has probably predisposed you—all of us, really—to have difficulty loving in a more unselfish way.

There is still one last principle that's absolutely critical for achieving success in your relationship. Early in the development of this model a major problem surfaced after working with many couples using the first three principles—love needs, changing NRPs, and using Softly Specific. Most people still had great difficulty in making real change; they lacked a stronger desire to really understand and go out of their way to meet the needs of their partner.

Their underlying belief system still rested upon the me-oriented self-centered approach to love that dominates our cultural thinking. There tended to be continuing complaints such as *I really don't have the time; I have too many other responsibilities; I have to take care of the kids,* or other concerns.

Consequently, couples often would fail to give the attention to remembering what the love needs of their partners were and wouldn't make it a priority to meet those needs. It was still too easy to become defensive and fall back into repeated conflict. Then the realization came to me that most couples really don't have a more developed belief system about romantic love and marriage that motivates and prepares them to love unselfishly.

So I've found there's still one final shift in thinking that is necessary to help couples be successful in applying these principles: They must place greater priority on the intentional goals of relationship improvement and loving one another more unselfishly. Without this shift in perspective, most couples tend to lack inspiration and interest for meeting the love needs of their partners. In my opinion, this is one of the biggest reasons why so many relationship difficulties exist today.

Self-Centered Love Dominates

The problem is that culturally transmitted concepts about relationships and marriage promote self-centered expectations about romantic love. Unselfish love does not receive enough emphasis. It's human nature to be relatively self-centered, especially in a me-oriented society. Most of the messages we get today reinforce a highly egocentric approach to romantic relationships. You feel "in love" because of the way a person looks, talks, and presents him or herself in personality. This elicits wonderful feelings of being in love because of what that person does for you.

This me-focused type of love pushes couples farther away from the simple solution to most of their relationship problems—unselfishly meeting one another's love needs.

The Projected Belief: You're Trying to Control Me!

Self-centered attitudes about romantic love set couples up for more conflict. Truly embracing a belief in the importance of unselfish love is essential for resolving conflicts, especially when using Softly Specific. Even when one partner delivers Softly Specific feedback in a very calm, respectful manner, there's still the possibility that the other partner may not be fully receptive, resent the change requests, or respond in an outright defensive manner.

This resistance is caused by a combination of self-centered beliefs about romantic love interacting with the deeply ingrained beliefs about not having to change behaviors when in a relationship: accept your partner for who he or she is; don't ask them to change. However, there is an additional belief, which immediately triggers defensiveness: *You're trying to control me!*

This projected over-concern about being controlled fosters defensiveness, keeping many couples locked in negative patterns. This self-sabotaging belief often involves the projection onto the partner that he or she is trying to control the other partner when asked to change behavior. It can be an almost automatic resistance. This is where the fourth principle becomes absolutely important, since it can help you avoid this natural defensiveness.

Principle #4:
Seek Relationship Self-Actualization and Altruistic Love

The fourth principle of the model was influenced by my experience in executive coaching, leadership development, and sales coaching. I found business clients generally highly motivated because they were dealing with their primary life goal: occupational-economic achievement. In fact, for some time it seemed to me that these individuals appeared to be more motivated and interested in making personal improvement in work performance than couples with marital problems were in making changes in their relationship. This led to the realization that the achievement of marital happiness is not given the same priority as work-related material success.

What I've found in working with couples is that this fourth principle is incredibly helpful for them when trying to resolve the issue of competing needs and avoiding conflicts. When the criteria for a couple dealing with any kind of relationship problem involves first always trying to carefully understand the needs of one's partner using unselfish love, it promotes an entirely different outcome. It's no longer *giving in* to your partner with a feeling that you were the one who had to compromise; rather it's *giving to* her or him unselfishly. This attitude will help tremendously in reducing conflict in your relationship.

This fourth principle reflects a values-driven marriage based on caring and consideration instead of self-centeredness. It calls for an expansion of society's generally accepted self-focused model of romantic love and marriage to include two key interrelated concepts:

1) Relationship self-actualization
2) Altruistic love

In this case the goal is, first, to achieve relationship self-actualization and, second, to achieve altruistic love. Until one truly internalizes these two beliefs, there will always be the possibility for partners to become defensive when asked to change behavior. And the tendency will be to interpret requests for change as controlling.

Here we use the term self-actualization in a more limited way than is generally used in theories of academic psychology. The term self-actualization has roots in humanistic psychology, most notably with Abraham Maslow. To avoid any theoretical debate about the validity of theories about self-actualization, we're going to use the term here in a more simplified way. The definition of self-actualization, according to Merriam-Webster's Eleventh Edition, is "to realize fully one's potential."

For our purposes, relationship self-actualization will be defined as the goal of achieving one's highest potential as a romantic partner or spouse, and the highest level of relationship success. Since altruism is generally accepted as a characteristic of self-actualization in many theoretical models of psychology, we similarly propose that altruistic love is the highest, most desirable type of love.

With this principle, you would choose to enter a romantic relationship with the specific desire of wanting to become a more unselfish, loving, self-actualized person. You would have the specific purpose of truly making your partner happy. But to clarify an important point: This is *not* a self-denying approach; rather it's a mutually altruistic relationship in which both partners seek to meet the important love needs of one another.

Taking Responsibility for Loving Your Partner Unselfishly

This moves the focal point of romantic relationships away from self-centeredness and represents a critical shift in calling for all of us to take full responsibility when entering any relationship for doing everything possible to meet the most significant emotional love needs of one's partner. That's a different way of looking at romantic love and marriage, isn't it?

Becoming the Best Romantic Partner

My first step in working with couples is to ask them if they have a goal to be the very best husband, wife, or romantic partner that they can possibly be. If so, does this have the same priority as their occupational-economic goal? Most say *no* to one or both questions. Likely you'll admit that attaining the highest level of achievement in your romantic relationship is not at the same level of priority as your job and financial goals. However, this is exactly what needs to happen.

Make The Shift In Your Thinking

Given all the busyness and stress of life, putting this principle into action on a daily basis can be difficult for most people. I often have clients—more often men—say to me that it's difficult to keep this in mind and they ask me for a trick or technique to help. So I tell them, here is the "secret technique"—it's really quite simple:

> You must want to become the best spouse or romantic partner and to hold this ideal at the same level of importance as your occupational and financial achievement. This means you think about it; you wake up in the morning and plan how you'll achieve this goal during the day in all your interactions with your partner. You watch yourself, monitor the NRPs you've committed to change, and ask for frequent feedback whenever you might fall off-track.

> Most importantly, you go out of your way to meet the unique emotional love needs of your partner at every opportunity. This is the "technique"! It's about making your romantic relationship a priority in life!

Having a burning desire to achieve greatness in your life as a romantic partner, husband, or wife provides motivation. It's becomes the driving force to find out what your partner's needs are to feel deeply loved, to remember them, and go the extra mile to actually meet those needs.

There is a measurement process to help you determine whether or not you've become an exceptional love partner and achieved a self-actualized relationship. You'll have accomplished this if your partner will be able to say to you, *Thank you. I feel so deeply loved and fulfilled in the relationship because you meet most of my love needs!* Remember, though, it's like anything else: If you don't have a goal, then you won't likely be successful in achieving it. Make relationship self-actualization and unselfish love a driving achievement goal in your life, and then you're bound to be successful.

Altruism Research and Marriage

There may be some skeptics who ask whether there's any proof that unselfish love will actually make a relationship more successful. Well, research says yes! Tom W. Smith, Ph.D., of the National Opinion Research Center at the University of Chicago, directed a study on altruistic love as part of the General Social Survey. Smith used data from the 2004 survey of 1,329 adults comparing it to the 2002 results.[19]

Smith determined that married people who express a high level of altruistic love toward their significant other turned out to have happier marriages. The study also showed that happiness for married people could be significantly increased if they have "this kind of self-sacrificing, put the interest of the other before my own interest, perspective on the romantic and close relationships," says Smith. In addition, altruistic love is a boon for all romantic relationships, even those that have not tied the knot. "Having feelings of altruistic love toward the significant other—a spouse, cohabitating partner, a simple romantic interest, which hasn't gone as far as either of those relationships—not only leads to greater marital happiness but increase in general happiness in one's life," Smith says.[20]

Unselfish Love: Going Out of Your Way

I'm sure there are going to be some saying that they don't want to have to do *everything* that their partner asks of them. If you have any such thoughts, don't worry. I suggest a simple proposal: go out of your way to understand what your partner needs to feel deeply loved and then try to actually fulfill those needs *at least to some major extent*. What this means is perhaps you may not do everything your partner wants. But you make a much greater effort to meet more of those needs, particularly those that are most important.

Thinking and behaving more unselfishly brings a refreshing approach to life that actually helps in reducing stress. When all we do is hash over our challenges day after day, we become self-absorbed. Loving others unselfishly actually gives an emotional release; it floods one with good feelings to see others happy and helps one feel better in general, as the Smith survey shows.

My Personal Example

I'll share a little about my own marriage. My wife likes to have a very clean and orderly house. I imagine she's in the upper 95-to-98 percent in the need to have things very clean—she might even be a little fussy. I'm only in the 60-to-65-percent when it comes to cleanliness. As you can guess, this offers many occasions where I'm just not up to her standards in keeping the house clean in the ways that would make her happy. So I have a choice of reacting negatively using the rationale of not wanting to be controlled, or I can go out of my way most of the time to keep things the way she likes them, out of altruistic love. I've chosen the latter, which she deeply appreciates.

Case Example:
From Hitting Rock Bottom to Awesome Love

A great example of the impact that commitment to a self-actualized marriage and unselfish love can have on a relationship is that of Sarah and Todd, a couple that have been together for seventeen years, since the age of fifteen, and married for nine years.

Before the first therapy session their relationship was at a point of desperation. Sarah later looked back and described it:

> We were both toxic, so angry, yelling, saying, *I hate you* in front of the kids. And in going for a walk with one another, rather than enjoying each other we would boil over. It was to the point we were both seriously considering separation.

There were major outside family pressures, overextension at work, and the stress resulted in hurtful behaviors. The initial work with this couple centered upon helping Sarah and Todd understand how they needed to seriously commit to having a self-actualized marriage and to unselfishly meet one another's love needs. They set this as a goal even though their lives were stressful and overextended and for too many years they had ignored their relationship. Both immediately took to embracing this commitment. They began to sincerely meet one another's love needs in such areas as trust, affection, intimacy, appreciation, and acknowledgment of feelings for one another. The transformation was really quite amazing. After eleven sessions, Sarah described the changes made in their relationship:

> For several months, just before coming in for the first session, we had hit rock bottom. I felt traumatized, like we tried everything, and the only thing to do would be to be done with the relationship. For those two months, we both had a real fear of divorcing and I was panicked that we were headed towards divorce.

However, Sarah said that now they were working together so they could both get love needs met, whereas in the past they had put those needs on the back burner. When asked how this affected their feelings towards one another, Sarah and Todd both said they felt there was a 90 percent increase in the level of positive romantic feelings. Further, they said conflict had been reduced from four or five times a week to only once during the previous month.

The change was remarkable. It was even visible in the verbal and physical affection they showed for one another, including the way they sat close, cuddled in the waiting room, and endearingly talked to each other in that session. When describing the change in their relationship, Sarah spontaneously turned to Todd and said:

> *Honey, your loving me this way now is so wonderful—it's awesome!*

Society Underdeveloped In Relationship-Marriage Skills

You may wonder why relationship self-actualization and altruistic love aren't given much attention in our culture. The reasons may relate to developmental stages in societal growth. Actually, in the psychological-social evolution of our society we're currently in a very primitive stage. Here we've lagged behind the technological and material advancement of society, which have proceeded at a much faster pace because they are the primary focal point of development.

It seems that the chief concern within western societies globally has been to achieve in the material area. Although there's nothing wrong with this, the area of human development involving relationship and marriage self-actualization has moved at a slower pace. In fact, we are *underdeveloped* in this area.

It's surprising to say that the US and other economically successful countries are underdeveloped in relationship and marital literacy skills for how to make a long-term relationship successful. This provocative assertion is supported by two facts: namely there is little education-training for how to be successful in marriage and there is a 50 percent failure rate of couples to maintain successful marriages and keep families intact. This reflects a social problem of the highest order with cascading repercussions. Yet it's so neglected.

Research on Decline in Values of Children

The reinforcement of self-absorbed cultural values regarding love in relationships may be starting in childhood at an early age. Research supports this concern. A 2011 study by UCLA psychologists reported in *Science Daily* found a rather dramatic, if not shocking, change in the values communicated in TV shows watched by children ages nine to 11 years old.[21] The study assessed the values of characters in popular television shows in each decade from 1967 to 2007. The results suggest that self-interested values in TV shows are on the rise while the values of benevolence and love for others are falling behind (See Appendix A for more details of this study).

Positive Culture Change—Self-Actualization and Altruism in Business

On the other hand, there is some *good* news regarding positive culture change and values! Interestingly, it's found in the area of business. A groundbreaking book, *Firms of Endearment,* by Raj Sisodia, Jag Sheth, and David Wolfe, asserts there's a whole new world in business which is positively affecting America's cultural evolution. The book indicates there's a burgeoning movement in business that focuses on feelings of a caring heart; a new age of empowerment and transcendence is driving society toward a higher cultural development. The authors say:

> The growing influence of self-actualization on mainstream culture is reshaping the way business is done. Indeed, it might be said that we are experiencing the beginning moments of the self-actualization of capitalism. More and more, companies are submerging their corporate egos, as it were, to focus more intensely on others—on their stakeholders, from customers and employees to suppliers, shareholders, and society at-large.[22]

The authors compared thirty humanistic "firms of endearment" to eleven companies classified as not just average but *great* in Jim Collin's book, *Good to Great.* The results showed that the thirty outperformed the eleven by 331 percent over a ten-year span of time![23] (See Appendix A for more details of the study.)

Growing interest in altruism is also shown in the recent New York Times bestseller: *Give And Take: Why Helping Others Drives Our Success.* Author Adam Grant is the youngest full professor and single highest rated teacher at The Wharton School. He cites research showing how "givers" are more likely than "takers" to be at the top of the business success ladder[24] and most people across 12 countries) rate giving as their single most important value[25].

In fact, Stefan Klein in his book *Survival of the Nicest* presents evidence that all of society has developed because of altruistic, rather than egocentric sentiment and will continue to evolve to higher levels because of it.

All of this suggests there may be a larger cultural movement of great significance occurring in our society promoting self-actualization and unselfish love for others, perhaps a new zeitgeist building energy for a positive values change.

Apply the Fourth Principle In *Your* Life

Culture change here will likely be slow; however you can choose right now to adopt these two transformational ideas of relationship self-actualization and altruistic love. And it can have huge impact on your relationship.

What I've found in working with couples is that after they consciously make real attempts to embrace this idea of self-actualization and altruistic love, they're inclined to be much less selfish. Big change begins to occur in a synergistic way. Both partners are more open to remembering the love needs of one another, fulfilling them, and paying attention to changing NRPs. When this occurs great things begin to happen in the relationship.

When you know that a partner isn't inclined to normally think of meeting a love need but goes out of their way to do so, it results in something remarkable. It's a special affirmation of love and connection, felt at the core of one's being. I've seen this happen with so many couples when making this shift in thinking to a more unselfish love. New feelings of joy and contentment are experienced.

The Thermostat Story

A couple in their seventh session described how the husband attempted to practice unselfish love with his wife in what they referred to as the "thermostat story." It was summertime and they were having an argument where he wanted the thermostat set at 68° while she wanted it at 72°. He said, "I'm normally contradictory and bull-headed, but I decided to really listen to her need more carefully." After hearing her reasoning, he decided to act unselfishly. He told her that it seemed that it was a more important need to her than it was to him, so he was going to go with her desire. She said at that moment it touched her so much she cried and said:

> Maybe you do love me. You tell me you do all the time but don't show it; this time I felt it. It felt so different; all my

resistance (she had acknowledged an emotional wall) fell away because you were thinking of me.

He responded further saying: *I want to get good at showing you.* She gave further positives about the change he was showing at home with both her and the children in listening to their needs and being less impatient or angry. He responded in an exceptionally articulate way:

It's enlightening to be in a relationship and approach day-to-day conflict with the idea of what your partner's needs are and thinking unselfishly about the other person's needs.

How to Love Less Selfishly

How would you become more unselfish in your love? It's quite simple—show daily commitment to looking for every opportunity to meet your partner's love needs. Try it as an experiment. Set the intention to pay more attention to meeting his or her love needs, then judge the response. I'm betting your efforts will be readily noticed and he or she will more likely respond back in a similar positive fashion. If you both keep doing this, it can change the nature of your relationship—taking it to a much deeper level of emotional connection, passion, and romantic feeling. Your relationship can become truly fabulous!

Integrating With Spiritual and Larger Life Beliefs

One thing I've found helpful for clients in adopting this new principle is to integrate it into one's religious or spiritual beliefs or philosophy of life. The way in which we have defined relationship self-actualization and altruistic love here can fit easily within whatever one's larger spiritual or philosophical beliefs might be. It doesn't matter whether you're religious, agnostic, or atheist.

The only requirement is that you desire to embody the personal characteristics and values of someone who demonstrates a higher form of love—altruistic love—for your romantic partner. And if you have religious or spiritual beliefs that encourage being loving and compassionate toward others, it should be easy to embrace this commitment. Developing unselfish love for others is a universally regarded spiritual goal of the highest order.

Perhaps the real test of our life beliefs, whether spiritual or nonspiritual, is the way we treat others, especially our romantic partners. So use your larger life beliefs to help inspire and motivate yourself to nurture unselfish love in your relationship.

Softly Specific Supports Self-Actualization

Another direct support for achieving relationship self-actualization and unselfish love is Softly Specific Co-coaching. The key psychological-interpersonal skills of a self-actualized person are actually already embedded within the six steps of Softly Specific:

- Empowered, nonaggressive, respectful assertiveness
- Ability to share emotionally vulnerable feelings
- Open, unbiased listening skill
- Empathy for feelings of others
- Emotionally secure in owning behavior; apologizing without excuses
- Capable of developing a deep emotional connection/love bond

Each one of these represents highly desirable attributes more likely to be found in self-actualized individuals. Softly Specific helps you acquire those characteristics. It also clears the path to actualizing yourself and relationship by better managing conflict.

Even when both partners practice unselfish love, they can easily fall back into derailing patterns of conflict sabotaging those efforts. It's tough for anyone to feel unselfish love when there is buildup from underlying hurt and anger caused by repeating conflict. This is another example of how each of the model's four principles is dependent on the other and operates synergistically.

Afraid You Can't Change? Yes, You Can!

After being presented with all four principles of the Relationship Co-Coaching model you might possibly be feeling a little hesitant, wondering if it's possible to learn these new skills. Don't worry; you're perfectly capable of change! However, you have to approach your marriage with a new attitude and take time to learn new things. This is a critical factor behind success. I've seen many couples with this commitment make change in their relationship using this model, and it surprised even me.

Essential Relationship Skills of Marriage

One of the things I've learned is that even as marriage therapists, we need to empower ourselves and not be afraid to ask clients to learn these skills. It's been exceedingly helpful for me to work as a psychologist both in business and in marriage counseling. I've come to believe more than ever in a performance skills learning approach if you want to become good at anything in life.

Specifically, success in any endeavor—leadership, sales, marriage, and parenting—depends upon setting a goal and making it a real priority. Then one proactively learns the skills to become successful. It just so happens that these skills for marriage are also important for all relationships, especially in work and business situations.

I've often observed a crossover of NRPs in marriage and in the workplace. A relational problem played out with co-workers may also be present in home life. A classic example is the wife who grows resentful of her husband being too dominating and authoritarian. In this case, I coach husbands not to talk to their wives in the same way they do others at work; I also suggest they may want to reassess using this style of leadership with co-workers!

One husband I worked with used the general principles of being softer and more specific not only with his wife, but also with his children and even others at work. He said that he has come to the realization of "I no longer have to raise my voice with anyone." The impact has been so profound for all his relationships; he referred to it as the Softly Specific "halo effect." I've repeatedly seen this with clients using the Softly Specific with their children and those in leadership positions applying it effectively in their workplace. See www.relationshipcocoaching.com for more to come on Softly Specific in parenting and leadership.

The bottom line is, whether at work or at home, if you want to change yourself then all you have to do is really commit to learning the key practices of whatever skills you want to develop! The four principles of the Relationship Co-Coaching model all build upon one another and can be used every day. These are foundational practices for cultivating deep love and happiness. Make relationship self-actualization and unselfish love a highest priority goal in your life; it will be the guiding principle and motivational force to help transform your relationship.

Self-Exploration Exercises

1) Do you have a goal for a self-actualized marriage that is equal or greater in importance to your job and financial achievement? If not, think about how you can make it so.
2) How unselfish is your love for your partner? In what ways could you be more altruistic in your approach to your partner?
3) Have you committed the specific love needs of your partner to memory and do you make every attempt on a daily basis to meet them?
4) Do you have a larger life belief or spiritual belief that would support you making a greater effort to love your partner more unselfishly? If so, exactly what are those beliefs and how might you use them to support internal change toward being more unselfish in your love?

You've now have all four principles of the Relationship Co-Coaching model. However, there are common obstacles and sabotage factors that can knock one off course even when following the model. The chapters in Section Two of the book will show you how to guard against these negative influences and keep them from derailing your own relationship.

The Relationship Co-Coaching Model for Dynamic Growth

1. Fulfill Partner's Love Needs
2. Identify and Change Negative Relationship Patterns (NRPs)
3. Reduce Conflict with Softly Specific Co-Coaching
4. Seek Relationship Self-Actualization and Altruistic Love

Section 2:
Common Relationship Barriers and Sabotage

Chapter 7

Three Sabotaging Beliefs Leading to Premature Break-Up

Why would you want to engage in a lifelong romantic relationship and risk crashing because you didn't want to bother to learn the skills to succeed?

By this time, it's evident that what's recommended requires a deliberate effort to develop and practice new skills. When couples in counseling realize this for the first time they usually express three common, interrelated concerns. These are important to mention because they are further variations of non-change societal beliefs. Each one represents negative assumptions that can sabotage change and contribute to premature dissolution of relationships.

Three Sabotaging Beliefs

Because one, two, or even all three of these beliefs might possibly be entering your mind or your partner's, let's consider these before going any further:

1) *I don't have the time that it will take to work on learning all these new relationship skills. I'm too busy with my job and other things.*
2) *Don't they say it's not possible to change one's personality?*

3) *I'm thinking it would just be easier to leave my partner since it's doubtful that I can change, or that he or she will either.* (This thought usually only occurs in relationships with more severe problems.)

Beliefs one and two typically contribute to the conclusion reached in number three. The best way to respond to these concerns is to share with you what I tell my clients when discussing these three negative beliefs.

I Don't Have Time to Learn New Skills

First, it does take time, like learning any new skill does. But the payoff is huge. The benefit is to improve your relationship. The problem is we have never learned the skills for how to make relationships successful so it's like we're now starting out taking "Relationship Skills 101."

When you wanted to learn to ride a bike, play a sport, play video games, play a musical instrument, cook, or anything else, it took time. There were specific behavioral skills you had to learn. Then you had to practice. It's exactly the same with relationships, especially marriage.

You can choose right now to learn the skills you need to have a successful relationship or you can continue on as you are, though that would seem to be a very illogical choice. If you were suddenly asked to pilot an airplane without any training, would you go ahead and do it? Most certainly not! Why would you want to engage in a romantic relationship and risk crashing because you didn't want to bother to learn the skills?

Actually, it really doesn't take much time. All you have to do is to remember what to say differently in handling conflict with your partner and to pay more attention to meeting his or her unique love needs. So it doesn't necessarily add more time to your day.

I Don't Think I Can Change

Regarding concern about "changing one's personality": you're not being asked to change your *entire* personality. Rather you're simply being asked to change some specific negative behaviors and learn new positive ones. Many couples have some derivation of this self-limiting belief: *But it would be so hard to change these habit patterns—I don't think I'm capable of doing it.*

Well, what if someone walked in your door a couple of days from now and told you that if you remembered to change those negative behaviors with your partner every single day for the next three months, you'd get a check for $10 million? Would you be able to be successful? I think so! So, you've answered the concern you have about whether you're really capable of changing your behavior. It's just a question of making it a priority in your life.

It May Be Easier for Me to Leave

This belief occurs primarily when there are more severe relationship problems. Please note that my response below does not pertain to cases where partners may be harmed or victimized by staying in certain situations such as abuse, alcoholism, addictions, infidelity, chronic lying, or other kinds of deception.

It *is* true that you certainly have the option of leaving your relationship. You do not have to put the work into it that's really needed to determine whether you and your partner can each change your negative relationship patterns (NRPs) and satisfy your love needs. However, remember that the NRPs pointed out by your partner will likely follow you into the future to whatever new relationship you develop.

After a time, the early stage of feeling wonderful in that relationship will also pass. You and your new partner will eventually transition into the same developmental stage where your NRPs will clash. Your options are to leave for a new relationship and postpone dealing with your NRPs, or you can proactively deal with them right now! Which would you rather do?

More often clients say that they'd rather deal with it now. This reasoning most often helps to alleviate concerns. And for couples with more severe problems wondering whether they should put the work in on the relationship or split up, most choose to proactively put in the work to at least giving the relationship a fair shot.

Yes, Love and Marriage Require Skills

In Relationship Co-Coaching you are being asked to consciously form new beliefs and actually practice new skills. It's quite possible that this may conflict with some of your previous conscious and subconscious beliefs about relationships.

It always seems so easy in the movies and on TV, doesn't it? And now you're being asked to look at love and marriage as a skill. That might be a little hard to consider. But think about this: Since every single role in life necessitates acquiring a skill, why wouldn't love and marriage?

Some people, especially women, share the belief during couples counseling that if they have to tell their partners what they need to feel loved, then the partner doesn't really love them. And if they have to coach their partner in practicing new skills, then it means that it's forced or artificial. Be careful; this line of thinking is false. It's really not a question of love; rather, it's a question of skills and cultural, gender-related role conditioning. Many people are not very skilled in expressing feelings of love to another, particularly men.

One of the most popular current relationship books—*Men Are from Mars and Women Are from Venus* by John Gray, PhD—points out these important differences between men and women. For example, Gray says the most frequent complaint of women is men "don't listen" offering solutions rather than giving empathy. One reason is their sense of self is so heavily derived from the ability to achieve results and successful accomplishment so they are focused on objects and things rather than feelings.[26]

While there may be basic hardwiring differences in gender, men have been so programmed to take on the traditional masculine role. They see their primary purpose as an economic provider, not one of sharing feelings or being more emotionally intimate in ways that women need. If you're a woman frustrated or unhappy with your husband not meeting your needs, don't give up hope or jump to conclusions. Please recognize that the man you're in a relationship with may be simply the victim of cultural conditioning. It may be necessary for him to learn some new behaviors such as empathetic listening in which he doesn't try to "fix" your feelings. This is one of the most common skills I teach husbands and their wives absolutely love it! However, just because he needs to learn new ways of relating does not mean that he doesn't already really love you.

Many Divorcing Couples Still Interested in Reconciliation

There is recent research that supports the point that couples may move too quickly into divorce mode. Dr. Bill Doherty, mentioned earlier for his work on the harmful effects of consumerism on marriage, has been one of the leaders in the working to prevent premature divorce. Doherty, along with Dr. Brian Willoughby and Bruce Peterson, JD, conducted a recent study that surveyed divorcing parents who were participating in required parenting classes.

The results are very interesting: Even after the divorce process was formally initiated, one partner (but not the other) indicated potential interest in reconciliation services in about one third of the divorcing couples. In about 10 percent of cases both partners had interest. In total, in about 45 percent of the divorcing couples, one or both spouses held some degree of belief that the marriage could be saved and would consider reconciliation help.[27]

These findings are extremely important. It suggests that a *substantial* number of couples may find themselves initiating divorce and following through with it *even though they still have interest in reconciliation*. What a tragedy, especially if some of these families could have been saved from the pain of divorce!

Dr. Doherty has developed a program, Discernment Counseling, which is aimed at helping couples where one of the spouses is *leaning out* (wanting to go) while the other is *leaning in* (wanting to stay). In this approach, the leaning out spouse explores whether to leave the marriage is the right decision and the leaning in spouse copes in a way that doesn't make the situation worse. Dr. Doherty used this approach with 25 couples, and 40 percent decided to attempt reconciliation.[28] This supports the assertion that many couples may prematurely divorce with insufficient effort made to reconcile using professional help.

Again, all of the above advice is not for cases where partners may be harmed or victimized by remaining in unstable or potentially dangerous situations.

When Is It Time to Divorce?

Frequently one or both partners in a troubled relationship are thinking very seriously of divorcing and wondering if couples counseling is even worth it. Often one partner is unhappier than the other and has communicated his or her needs in the past with little or no response. Years of frustration and resentment end up severely damaging feelings of romantic love. Unfortunately, many couples wait far too long before getting help, which may cause one or both partners to view divorce as the easiest, best option. In this case, the three self-limiting negative beliefs above are present in full force.

Occasionally I talk with partners who are at this extreme point of frustration and are ready to end the relationship. My typical counter-responses to the three negative beliefs may not be enough. They still may be very skeptical about beginning the work of marriage counseling, especially if they've had one or more failed therapy attempts in the past. I say this to these couples:

> Do not prejudge and assume your partner is a poor fit for you just because you've had so many years of frustration. I'm not trying to tell you that your partner is or is not the right one for you, or that you should ultimately stay with your spouse, or divorce them. I am just saying that you should give marriage therapy a try. If not, you'll never know whether your partner really is good for you.

You may think your partner cannot change. However, you may never have been through couples therapy directly focused on changing behavior. You don't really know what would happen. What if you both made the commitment to unselfishly meet each other's love needs and change negative relationship patterns? It could change the entire course of your marriage.

I've been surprised in seeing the change that some partners make after using this model. I can understand one might feel pessimistic after so much hurt and frustration over such a long time, however one won't really know whether a relationship can be renewed until giving it a try.

Couples frequently ask me how to know when enough is enough and that divorce is okay. I advise them to embrace this whole model in couples therapy and sincerely try to create change. Use the renewed effort as a way to further evaluate the relationship to determine whether to stay with it. Engage in the process diligently for at least a few months. Clearly identify love needs and negative relationship patterns. Give it your all. Then you can honestly say that you've gone out of your way to meet the love needs of your partner, and you've changed your own negative behavior patterns. If your partner has failed to do so for you, then you have every right to leave. What I've found, though, is that in many cases couples are able to entirely turn around their relationship, restoring love and happiness.

Give It Everything You Possibly Can

Using this logic is often the tipping point for getting clients to commit to giving it one last try. And it's amazingly gratifying to see many of these relationships renewed through using the Co-Coaching model.

As you can see, the purpose here is to help you guard against making self-limiting assumptions about what you can achieve in your marriage. Some couples may prematurely divorce while others with less severe problems may assume they need to accept mediocrity instead of revitalizing their marriage. Don't limit your relationship! Take the time first to go through this kind of change-oriented process to see whether you can create a relationship more satisfying than you might ever have thought possible.

While clearly this is a call for advocacy for strengthening the institution of marriage, it's not a blind recommendation that anyone stay in an unhappy marriage. Rather, it encourages an intelligent, educated approach. If you're considering divorce, do everything possible to make the best decision before dissolving a relationship, especially when children are involved. If the breakup of a family can be avoided through marital renewal, then fight for it!

Although you may not be in the more serious situation of considering leaving a relationship, examine whether any of these three sabotaging beliefs are currently causing you to accept less than what you deserve in a relationship.

Self-Exploration Exercises

1) Have you been influenced by any of the big three sabotaging beliefs outlined in this chapter? Determine if any of these beliefs listed below are causing you to doubt or question your relationship:

    a. *I don't have the time that it will take to work on learning all these new relationship skills. I'm too busy with my job and other commitments.*
    b. *Don't they say it's not possible to change one's personality?*
    c. *I'm thinking it would just be easier to leave my partner since it's doubtful that I can change, or that he or she will either?* (For more severe marital problems.)

2) If you've been biased by any of these beliefs, in what ways has this kept you from putting more effort into improving the relationship?
3) Depending upon which of the three negative beliefs have influenced you, consider the counter-logic below for each of these three beliefs respectively:

    a. You are *not* too busy and *can* make the time, when you make it a priority.
    b. It is indeed possible to change any behavior that you want in a relationship.
    c. Don't give in to fears that you or your partner can't change! Move ahead with marriage therapy that's actively focused on changing negative relationship patterns.

Unselfishly meet your partner's love needs and learn new skills for reducing conflict.

Next, we'll discuss another factor with the potential for causing serious harm to a relationship: an affair. The next chapter will be devoted to this issue, how to heal the emotional pain, and how to prevent an affair from ever happening.

The Relationship Co-Coaching Model for Dynamic Growth

1. Fulfill Partner's Love Needs
2. Identify and Change Negative Relationship Patterns (NRPs)
3. Reduce Conflict with Softly Specific Co-Coaching
4. Seek Relationship Self-Actualization and Altruistic Love

Chapter 8

The Affair and Its Complications— How to Avoid It!

Given the right set of circumstances, relationship unhappiness combined with lack of boundaries can set up vulnerability to an affair.

One of the most painful experiences for any spouse is the discovery of an affair. Let's take a look at affairs, how to avoid them, and what can be done when they do occur. The impact of an affair can be huge, causing enormous pain that's difficult to heal. Couples whose marriages have been shaken by an affair may appreciate further insight as to how to deal with it. There may even be some readers questioning whether they want to stay in a relationship after one.

In order to avoid the possibility of an affair ever happening, it's important to understand the dynamics of what sets a couple up for the possibility. There are influencing factors that create vulnerability, which all couples need to guard against. It's important to protect the sanctity of one's relationship over the long-term. Once an affair occurs it becomes a major roadblock, posing a challenge for any marriage. The effect is destructive—foundational trust is damaged. The spouse who has been hurt experiences devastating feelings of insecurity. Even an affair, though, is not necessarily insurmountable.

There are a number of related causes for affairs: weak values, relationship unhappiness, lack of boundaries in friendships, and alcohol or drugs. All it takes is one or more to set the stage for an affair. When multiple factors are present, the risk is greater. Any partner can become susceptible to an affair, especially if deep feelings of hurt and resentment have built up over time from unmet love needs and harmful NRPs.

Affairs Caused by Lack of Strong Morals

In one particular kind of affair, however, there may be deeply rooted character flaws. Some individuals may not have any real interest in changing their behavior; they may simply lack strong values regarding fidelity. I worked with one couple in which the husband had an affair and was confronted by his wife in the session. I supported her expressed need to have his total commitment to fidelity in their marriage. He responded defensively, saying that no man could really promise faithfulness in every situation.

In fact, he then challenged me personally, saying, "What would you do if while on a business trip, [a famous actress] walked naked into your hotel room and wanted to have sex with you?" I responded by saying that I would decline, because it was against my values. That client refused to believe me and actually continued to argue, saying that I was "fooling myself."

Obviously, this is an example of someone who lacks strong values regarding fidelity to the point that he projected his loose morals onto every other man, assuming they would all behave in the same way he would. With these kinds of affairs, the lack of strong values about fidelity must be confronted head-on. If a genuine change in values does not occur within the unfaithful spouse, the deceived partner will be taking a huge risk by staying in the marriage.

Marital Unhappiness and Cultural Beliefs Can Lead to Affairs

Unlike the above situation, however, an affair can occur without issues regarding questionable values. I've talked with many couples where the betrayed spouse said it was totally shocking to discover the affair because of previously voiced values by the cheating partner regarding fidelity. Now, we can certainly debate how strong the values were in the first place because, after all, an affair did occur. But I've found with many of these couples there was a prolonged buildup of negative feelings and marital unhappiness stemming from unmet love needs and the NRP chain reaction of hurt and anger.

Unfortunately, society's beliefs can also predispose couples to affairs. There's little education for couples to help them anticipate and prepare for encountering NRPs, or how to change those negative patterns. Cultural messaging frequently focuses upon themes of affairs, giving tacit acceptance. Consequently, there's little, if any, realistic expectation regarding the degree of communication and personal change needed to ensure a successful long-term romantic relationship.

As noted previously, marriage is often viewed with a static non-growth mindset of "accept me just as I am." These erroneous beliefs contribute to unhappy marriage partners assuming their spouses will never change. This causes them to accept unhappiness in the marriage, doing nothing about it, making them more vulnerable to having an affair when presented with the right set of circumstances.

Case Example: Assumption That Relationships Can't Change

I worked with a couple having severe relationship problems but without the complication of an affair. The husband came only reluctantly to the first two sessions, adamant that the relationship was "beyond repair." He had made the direct threat to his wife that if she did not change, he would not continue in a loveless marriage and would seek affection in an outside sexual relationship.

This is a perfect example of how a spouse who feels hopeless will justify an affair. The husband in this case became hopeful for the first time after his wife made agreements to fulfill his desire to be loved in ways he'd wanted after years of feeling despair.

The influence of these beliefs runs deep. Unhappy partners frequently question whether they really have the right to ask their spouse to change and are prone to thinking they should be doing a better job of "accepting" their partner.

Chain Reaction: Hurt, Anger, and Susceptibility to an Affair

Subsequently, hurt and anger may continue to be suppressed regarding unmet love needs with NRPs growing stronger over time. The result often is gradual diminishing of the feeling of romantic love and emotional connectedness. Disappointment or despondency may occur. When this happens, there is typically serious questioning about whether someone is with the right person or in the right marriage. This can lead to feelings of being trapped in the marriage with no way out. All of this further promotes hopeless acceptance of an unhappy situation.

Obviously, this negative chain reaction does not always progress to the severity where one begins to feel complete despair. It's not uncommon for someone in a relationship to occasionally go through periods where some or even all of the above feelings are experienced, at least to some degree. It's natural to get upset with your partner for not meeting love needs and recurring NRPs, and to feel frustrated when that partner doesn't change.

However, this discontent can become a much deeper source of marital unhappiness, potentially making one vulnerable to an affair. So one must be vigilant regarding any feelings of resentment and hurt that occur in marriage and proactively take steps to address those issues. The ability to let go of minor annoyances and nitpicking is important. However, ignoring or minimizing the buildup of major feelings of hurt, anger, or resentment relating to important issues can be very dangerous for a marriage.

When an Affair Happens

For those couples where an affair has occurred, first get help from a marriage therapist. Many couples are able to successfully navigate the rough waters of an affair, going on to experience an even happier marriage. When counseling couples where there has been an affair, I take the following approach: First and foremost, the partner who has been hurt must receive support and validation for his or her pain and feelings of mistrust.

After an affair, unfaithful partners typically want to move beyond it as soon as possible, often expressing frustration and anger at the spouse for continuing to bring it up. However, it's natural for the betrayed to experience after-effects of the affair—a wound has been created for which continued healing is necessary. They often need to revisit it, know details about it, and understand why it happened. This can create conflict in the relationship because the guilty partners want to avoid continued exposure to the emotional pain they've caused and their own personal guilt and shame.

Boundary Violations Can Lead to Affairs

In looking at how to protect one's relationship let's consider the issue of boundary violations in affairs because it's very important for the long-term security of any relationship. It's safe to say that in every instance of an affair there has been a failure to maintain stricter boundaries regarding friendships. Many affairs happen when one partner begins to confide in a friend about marital difficulties.

When sharing significant feelings of any type—especially dissatisfaction in your marriage—with someone else that is potentially a romantic partner, an emotional connection can occur. Attraction may gradually surface, and subsequently there is greater susceptibility to an affair. This is particularly true when alcohol is involved, which serves as a dis-inhibitor. Given the right set of circumstances, relationship unhappiness combined with lack of boundaries can set up vulnerability to an affair.

Preventing the Affair

All of these situations need to be strictly guarded against by you and your partner to protect the fidelity of the relationship. That's why it's so important to have clear, mutually agreed-upon protective guidelines for how to handle friendships. Loyalty and faithfulness to one's partner are values that must be nurtured and supported by strong boundaries.

In addition, if you both accept this model's four principles for relationships, it will also help. If you each genuinely make it a priority in your life to meet your partner's love needs unselfishly and change your own NRPs, there will be much less likelihood for an affair due to deeper love and happiness in the marriage.

Hope For Recovering From an Affair

If you're in a relationship where an affair has occurred marital therapy can be of great help (see therapeutic approach offered in *Appendix C*). Exploring the love needs and NRPs causing marital unhappiness may offer helpful psychological insight and motivation to create a happier, more satisfying marriage. Many couples go through their healing process and develop an even happier relationship than they had before the affair.

There is reason for great hope even if an affair has occurred (except with partners unwilling to commit to fidelity). But it does take a great deal of work and commitment—without a doubt it's absolutely worth it to at least give it a try!

Self-Exploration Exercises

If you are someone dealing with the aftereffects of an affair, be sure that you seek professional help.

For those interested in proactively protecting their relationship from the possibility of an affair, have an open conversation with your partner conducting a personal audit regarding key vulnerability factors:

1) Potential weakness in values regarding fidelity.
2) Underlying marital dissatisfaction that hasn't been dealt with regarding harmful NRPs or unmet love needs.
3) Lack of strict boundaries with outside friendships.
4) Use of alcohol or drugs that offer the potential to loosen inhibitions.

Last, decide upon a clear set of mutually agreed-upon boundaries for friendships with others.

In the next chapter, we'll explore one of the biggest barriers to relationship happiness. It's something we all are familiar with and do battle with every day: too much stress in our lives.

The Relationship Co-Coaching Model for Dynamic Growth

1. Fulfill Partner's Love Needs
2. Identify and Change Negative Relationship Patterns (NRPs)
3. Reduce Conflict with Softly Specific Co-Coaching
4. Seek Relationship Self-Actualization and Altruistic Love

Chapter 9

Managing Stress In Relationships

Are you feeling overly tired, keyed up, or tense too much of the time? If so, you should carefully assess whether you're being sucked into a self-created vortex of pressure.

Any book on marriage would not be complete without addressing stress. If you look up stress in the dictionary, synonyms include: pressure, strain, anxiety, tension, and worry. Each of these can affect the quality of romantic relationships. We all have many responsibilities and feel pressure to succeed. It's easy for stress to exact its toll on our bodies and minds. The question for you is how much stress is hurting your relationship? And in what ways?

Under this continual tension, we all have a choice to make at critical moments in the way we interact with our partners—and children. It may be that we are having a bad day and feeling irritable because of frustrating circumstances. Later that day, during a busy evening of fixing dinner or taking care of the kids, our partner may flippantly say something to us that we really don't care for.

At that moment we have a decision to make. We can respond with irritability, terseness, or some other negative response. An argument may then occur and the evening begins with hurt feelings and resentment, which can last for a few minutes, an hour, the night, or even a day or more. Or we can choose to react in a more respectful, constructive way, perhaps expressing your feelings with Softly Specific. Doing so can make all the difference in the world. At numerous points of interaction during the day, each of us has an opportunity to handle feelings in a way that will enable the relationship to run smoothly or set it up for tension and conflict.

Stress Most Often is Mental

The source of our stress is most always internal. In fact, one of the best definitions of stress is *it is our perception of threat to self or self-esteem*. Stress involves an interpretive reaction to the events around us. Recognizing this can give an added sense of control. If you know that it's always about the way you react internally, then you have the potential to substantially reduce stress of any type by the way you choose to view it.

This presents moment-to-moment decisions to change our perceptions; it's how we process the many different stressful situations in life. Each of these moments presents the opportunity for learning how to maintain calm during difficult circumstances. We have the choice to reframe external circumstances in a way that de-escalates the internal perception of threat.

This approach for reducing stress through mental reframing can be particularly relevant when applied to relationships. Quite simply, much of the stress experienced in relationships comes from expectations. We expect to be treated a certain way so when we're not treated that way, we emotionally react. The Relationship Co-Coaching model and its four principles can be a huge help in reducing stress. It offers an entirely different way to respond to partners when something upsetting happens.

Reduce Stress by Expecting Imperfections

You can now entertain a more realistic belief about what to expect in relationships. Namely, one's partner will indeed do and say things, sometimes frequently, that have the potential to be upsetting. So, be ready to give respectful Softly Specific feedback. Also recognize that, as discussed earlier, we all have core emotional grievances maintained by generalized beliefs. When our partner engages in certain negative behaviors generalized grievances can be activated, triggering hurt and possibly anger.

Why not recognize these grievances as a set-up? These are our own self-generated reactions causing stress. Instead, reframe the way we look at the situation when our partner does something potentially upsetting. Expect it to happen—no one is perfect.

Given this reality of relationships, let's work on not getting so upset with a partner. It won't be overlooking or excusing the behavior in question since you'll be assertive and empowered through Softly Specific.

Develop Self-Control Regarding Emotional Grievances

How does one stop from getting upset? Find new patterns of calming self-talk when a partner engages in those negative behaviors. Tell yourself, *I'll just remain calm and share my feelings using Softly Specific. There's no need to get angry.* This certainly can be challenging, however we can learn to modify our emotional reactions.

We all are culturally conditioned to move way too quickly from vulnerable feelings of being hurt, sad, or disappointed and upshift to feelings of anger. Instead, learn to pause and identify the vulnerable feelings. Then share these feelings with your partner using Softly Specific. Doing this will help reduce one of the major stressors in life: relationship conflict. With all that happens in a day, our romantic relationships need to be a safe haven. Applying the Co-Coaching principles is one of the best stress management techniques you ever learn.

Stress Created By Overextension

This is an all too common problem in many relationships: the stress from having too much to do—being way too busy. When working with clients, I always recommend attempting to reduce stress in the relationship by stepping back and looking at the big picture to determine what's really important. We all feel pressure to be successful in so many areas with the overriding goal often being financial achievement.

The societal mentality of excessive consumerism propels us toward compulsive overextension to keep up with materialistic expectations. Interestingly, the United States is one of the most affluent countries in the world. However, it's also one of the few places where people with a relatively high standard of living still tend to do everything themselves: cooking, cleaning, gardening, and shuttling kids to activities. In many other countries, these are daily tasks for which others are often employed, but in the U.S., many could actually afford it by better budgeting, but instead do all of these things themselves.

Rebelling Against Perfectionistic Society

When first confronting clients with the idea that they may be continually overextending, I suggest that we are all victims of a perfectionistic society pushing us to do too much. The resistance I hear is, *I think you're right; I just wish I had the money so I could pay for some of these other things!* If this is your initial reaction, too, I invite you to consider that the shortage of money is most likely self-imposed. It ultimately relates to choices made in priorities relating to what we choose to spend money on.

There's a tendency for many of us to push ourselves financially to do it all: purchase the largest house or car, send children to private school, go on expensive vacations, and more. There may not be room in the budget for outsourcing selected tasks to others. The first step is to guard against financial overextending. Perfectionistic beliefs that one should do it all can result in our quality of life suffering. Stress from overextension can cause your thoughts to race and to feel less enjoyment in life.

The first thing is to set up a new expectation: Guard against taking on too many outside responsibilities. Curb the tendency to try and do too much. Budget for lawn service, snow removal, housecleaning, and home remodeling projects. This is particularly crucial when both partners are working and have limited time together for themselves and their children. Why waste time on household tasks when time with loved ones is so scarce? Try to plan for outsourcing at least some household jobs so you can place priority on a better quality of life. If you don't consciously do this, it's highly unlikely to happen.

Too Many Outside Activities

This same advice holds true for overextension from outside activities that affect you and your children. Whether it's doing too much for volunteer organizations, hobbies, sports, or home projects, one must be careful. These may be enjoyable activities, but balance is the key. Are you feeling overly tired, keyed up, or tense too much of the time? If so, carefully assess whether you're being sucked into a self-created vortex of pressure—become highly vigilant when taking on outside activities to ensure that quality of life doesn't suffer.

If you have children, protect them also. The demands have become equally great for them as well, with pressure to become involved in many extracurricular activities such as sports, music, cheerleading, dance, gymnastics, and debate, all starting at very young ages. Activities can be beneficial, but be aware when it becomes too much. Rebel against society's perfectionistic tendencies to overextend. Set priorities and protect the quality of your life. After achieving this balance between family, work, and activity, look for additional ways to manage stress, such as exercise and enjoying a healthy diet.

Fun and Enjoyment Reduce Stress

Take time each day to do things that are relaxing and enjoyable. This is one of the best antidotes for stress. Enjoyment helps offset the harmful physiological and psychological effects of stress. It's a fundamental, vitally important element of stress management.

Yet so many people fail to take this time, often because of overextension. The answer again relates to better prioritization. When clients tell me they just can't afford the time, I suggest that even if they can find just 20 minutes each day it will be well worth it to help reduce stress and being more relaxed, and potentially creating a better mood when relating to partners and children.

I use this logic particularly with women who are overwhelmed with responsibilities in raising children, especially if they are working outside the home. Often women feel they can't afford to take time for themselves. It seems they find it difficult to give themselves permission to do something enjoyable or rejuvenating. If you happen to be one of these women, please take the time! Reduce overextension and look for ways that your partner can help support you taking time every day to re-energize. Sometimes this may involve asking one's husband to take more involvement in some of the nightly duties, helping with the children, or other household responsibilities.

This is especially important if you are a woman experiencing ongoing feelings of resentment about your husband not taking on his fair share of domestic and child caring activities. The demands placed on women are greater than ever. Unfortunately a recent study shows women still do two-thirds of the housework.[29] It's important for women to ask for help in restoring balance in these everyday tasks.

While it seems to be more difficult for women, it's also hard for men to take time. If you're reluctant, try an experiment. First take just fifteen to thirty minutes every evening for one week to do something enjoyable or relaxing. See how you feel, how it affects the quality of your interactions with loved ones. Whether it's reading, sports, exercising, taking a warm bath, taking dance, yoga, tai chi class—just take the time. Even if you don't feel like you can take the time, do it for your loved ones. They'll appreciate the impact that it can have on the way you relate to them!

Self-Exploration Exercises

Perform a stress analysis in all of the below areas with your partner. Identify specific ways you want to change and help each other follow through in making changes in these areas.

1) Look for any areas of overextension in your life. Are there opportunities to eliminate some activities or to better prioritize your time? Guard against tendencies to overextend and target areas to change.
2) Look for any and all ways that you can outsource home responsibilities to free up time: housecleaning, lawn care, snow removal, cooking, and more. Pay to outsource tasks whenever possible.
3) Ask yourself how much time you take each day to do things that are relaxing and enjoyable. Build in at least 10 to 15 minutes a day. Remember, this is one of the best ways to reduce stress.
4) Consider carefully how to reduce stressful conflict in your relationship by *expecting* some imperfection from your partner. Look for areas of suppressed resentment regarding generalized core emotional grievances, NRPs, and unmet love needs. Then make sure to use Softly Specific rather than letting stressful feelings build up. Remember, nobody enjoys being around a grumpy, tense person. Becoming a more relaxed and

happier person will make you a better, more loving romantic partner—and parent!

We've now completed Section 2 of the book regarding predictable blocks to achieving relationship happiness. Next, we'll move to Section 3 showing how to create and sustain deep positive feelings of love over many years of marriage.

The Relationship Co-Coaching Model for Dynamic Growth

1. Fulfill Partner's Love Needs
2. Identify and Change Negative Relationship Patterns (NRPs)
3. Reduce Conflict with Softly Specific Co-Coaching
4. Seek Relationship Self-Actualization and Altruistic Love

Section 3:
Love Deepening Skills for Closeness, Affection, and Romance

Chapter 10

Building In the Four Types of Relationship Closeness

One of the most important ways to connect is through taking time for sharing and talking—conversational intimacy.

This section of the book deals with vital practices to help deepen love and personal connection in your relationship. One of the first places to start is how you spend time together. This is especially important given the busyness of life. One big problem with couples who come in for counseling is that they have made other things in life more important than their relationship. Often they have neglected one or more of the four types of closeness in a relationship. Why does this happen so often?

The reason typically relates to the issues of stress already discussed. The culture we currently live in is a potential pressure cooker. It's a highly perfectionistic society with everyone trying to do too much. We tend to overextend ourselves. Jobs, children, and other responsibilities too often come ahead of the relationship.

Allowing this to happen can be a mistake. Once a couple begins to spend less time together, it's easier to fall back into negative feelings of hurt and resentment leading to increasing emotional distance.

When working with couples in counseling, I often see a fundamental neglect of the relationship. They are not spending enough time together just talking, enjoying one another's company, and having fun. The addition of negative feelings from conflict contributes to couples becoming accustomed to being less close, less loving, and more distant. Other priorities like children, work, and even outside friendships can become more important than the relationship. If the distance becomes too great, it can spell real trouble for the relationship.

Unresolved Conflict and Lack of Closeness

One notable cause for lack of closeness is conflict. Much of this book shows how to more effectively manage conflict, so before going any further an important point must be made. Everything presented in this chapter is based upon the assumption that one has been proactive in determining whether any underlying feelings of hurt or resentment from conflict are causing lack of closeness and connection.

If so, these negative feelings must first be addressed (refer to the earlier chapters on NRPs and Softly Specific Co-Coaching). Trying to restore closeness in the ways recommended here can accelerate healing from conflict. However, attempting to rebuild closeness back into the relationship without addressing underlying issues of conflict may end in failure.

The Four Types of Closeness

Now let's explore how taking the time to build in opportunity to be close and connect is essential sustenance for the relationship. Take a look at the four ways to be close in a relationship, and consider how you and your partner fare in:

1) Conversational intimacy
2) Shared interests and activities
3) Physical affection
4) Sex

Conversational Intimacy

One of the most important ways to connect is through taking time for sharing and talking, conversational intimacy. Now there can be a potential gender difference here; women tend to have a greater need to communicate and share feelings compared to men. Although this is a generalization, it is more often women who complain about men not talking enough and sharing feelings with them. Regardless of gender, building in this time is extremely important.

If taking time to talk in your relationship has suffered, here are some things you can do. First, build back in more time for conversation—make it a ritual of spending at least 10 to 15 minutes or more talking about each other's day. Discuss not only issues at work or in home life, but also current events, and areas of mutual conversational interest.

Having a busy life is not a good excuse to neglect taking this time. Intentionally create the opportunity—set aside time, even if it's just a few minutes here and there during the evening. The first step is to realize how important conversational intimacy is to your relationship, and then make it a priority. For example, take that time as you drive children to activities or as you sit together watching them participate. Find pockets of a few minutes here and there to talk. Maybe it's after your partner comes home from work, a few minutes during dinner, afterwards when clearing dishes, or just after the kids go to bed.

Remember, you must be very proactive and creative to build in these moments to talk. So many couples tell me they don't take enough time for this. If you're waiting for a fifteen-minute stretch of clear uninterrupted time, it may never happen! And while this seems obvious, many clients say they rarely take this time!

Finding Time to Talk in My Marriage

My wife and I lead fast-paced lives, but we love those moments when we're able to talk with one another. And sometimes we have to be more flexible when so busy. Although we do take time every day to talk in a relaxed way, there are times when one of us is in the middle of something, possibly even moving quickly from one part of the house to another. In this circumstance, the busier one lets the other know the only way to talk will be in motion so the other will tag along and talk to the one working on other things.

My wife and I may have a busy day ahead with not much time to talk. If I happen to have a free moment in the morning while she's getting ready for the day, I'll come into the bathroom and sit down on the floor against the wall to chat with her as she does her hair and makeup. She absolutely loves for me to do it, knowing that I'm going out of my way just to be with her.

Assessing Your Conversational Closeness

It takes this kind of creativity to make time for one another. So the question is, how much time do you and your partner take every day to talk with one another? And what do you talk about? Do you share enough about your day and what's happened? Do you enjoy mutual interests?

For example, do you talk about the people and relationship issues in your workplaces? Do you talk about current national and world events? Do you have enough in common? These are all important areas to explore with your partner to see where you might improve your level of conversational intimacy.

Shared Interests and Activities

Next, let's discuss the second area of closeness in a relationship: shared interests and activities. You may recognize the overlap with conversational intimacy since shared interests and activities provide you with topics of mutual interest you can talk about; enhancing mutual interests can also improve conversational closeness.

This second area of closeness is one that many couples neglect. You are fortunate if you and your partner have many mutual interests. That's not the case in many relationships. It should also be noted here that having children certainly qualifies as a big area of mutual interest, though obviously a relationship needs more than just this. With all the stress in life, it's easy for a couple to neglect taking time to nurture common interests and activities. Once again, this may require you going outside of your comfort zone.

On occasion, I'll have husbands who say *Well, my wife doesn't like to do any of the activities that I love, which are watching sports, hunting, and fishing.* In this case, I suggest that perhaps they are being a tad bit unrealistic in expecting that their wives would want to engage in these stereotypically male activities.

Brainstorm for New Interests

My prescription for couples is to brainstorm for interests or activities. This may involve some stretching for each person. How about taking up bicycling, rollerblading, tennis, or golf? Or how about trying out painting or drawing, yoga, tai chi, a book club, attending special artistic/sports events? Maybe it's a date night, dinner and a movie on a regular basis. Many couples enjoy cooking together and make time on a Saturday evening to have a special romantic dinner. And for some busy couples, it's making time to watch favorite TV shows together and snuggle next to each other on the couch. Most people just don't try out enough new activities, so explore new directions. Talk with your partner and discuss whether you think there are sufficient shared interests and activities in your relationship. Add adventure to your life and try new things!

Physical Affection

We're not talking sex here. It's physical affection—hugs, kisses, playful touches that bring you closer to each other. This is the third area of closeness often neglected by couples caught in the fast pace of life. It's actually one of the most important ways to maintain a deeper love bond. What I've found in working with couples is not that they don't want to be more affectionate; rather it's something that is just easy to forget.

The type of affection preferred may be unique to each person and often relates to love needs. What is the form of touch and affection that helps you and your partner feel most deeply loved? This is an important question for you both to explore.

It's so easy to fall away from the levels of physical affection present in the early stage of falling in love. Couples need to pay attention to keeping affection alive throughout the many years of a relationship. Take action now to find out what you both can do to keep affection strong in your relationship.

In this exploration, it's important to be very specific in defining what it is that you like from your partner. How do you like to be embraced, kissed, snuggled? How would you like to be given a back, neck, or foot massage? These desired forms of affection often also represent significant love needs.

Part of this conversation also needs to include discussion regarding how to gently communicate to one another when you might not be feeling the need to be physically close.

Remembering to be affectionate with your partner in ways they most desire will always be appreciated. The power of physical touch is great; it helps promote emotional connection and romantic feelings.

Sexual Closeness

The fourth expression of closeness in a romantic relationship is sex. While there is a societal over-focus on sexuality—one might even say we have a hypersexual culture—having a rich sexual relationship is very important for any couple. Actually, sex can be neglected just as much as the first three types of closeness. As a relationship progresses people become overly familiar with one another. We need to be proactive to keep the sexual relationship interesting, exciting, and fulfilling. There are several problems that can confront couples in their sex life.

First, there's the issue of simply taking time for sex, making it a priority. Long work hours, children, and other stressors can all add up to not paying enough attention to the sexual relationship. These real concerns can deplete personal energy and distract couples from sex. These are potential barriers that everyone should anticipate in a long-term relationship and take preventative action to keep sex alive and well.

Remember—Negative Emotions Affect Sexual Desire

And as noted previously, let's not forget that negative feelings can affect desire for sex regardless of gender. Build-up of hurt or resentment can directly impact interest for sex and being emotionally connected. Nobody wants to talk as much, be as affectionate, or act lovingly with someone for whom they have underlying negative feelings.

In fact, it's not just women whose sexual feelings are affected by emotions. This can also hold true for men. It's not uncommon for me to work with couples where the wife is surprised to hear that the husband has lost interest sexually because of hurt or angry feelings relating to the way she has treated him. It may seem difficult for some wives to believe, especially if they've held to an assumption that men always want sex and don't have to be in the mood.

Once again we see the importance of addressing any negative feelings upfront using Softly Specific, so the desire to be emotionally or physically connected does not diminish.

Be Creative in Finding Opportunity

Finding time for sex is often an issue for many couples, especially those with children. This is especially true for couples with three or four children, which is an enormous amount of responsibility. These parents often tell me that they just don't have the opportunity to have sex. It's hard for them to have even a brief period of time where they're not afraid the children will knock on the door and interrupt them so they rarely have sex.

My advice to couples with children around the house is to be creative. I've suggested that if it's actually true that given the age of their children and frequency of interruptions they really can't have sex then they have to be innovative. For example, hire a babysitter who takes all of the children out to Chuck E. Cheese for a few hours on a Friday or Saturday night. This gives the couple intimate time together and afterwards they can go out to dinner and have a date night.

Or for those who can't afford a babysitter, an alternative would be to trade off babysitting with the parents of children who are friends with your kids to free up a weekend date night. Also, children often really look forward to an overnight with grandparents, leaving an entire night for a couple to enjoy each other's company.

Whether any of these suggestions is the exact solution for you isn't the point; rather, it's to encourage you to keep your sexual relationship a priority and make the effort to keep it strong. Another concern often expressed by couples is reluctance to schedule sex into their week because of the perception that it takes all the spontaneity away. My response to these couples is that if they don't schedule it, then like many things in our busy lives, it's unlikely to happen!

Identifying days and times during the week as windows of opportunity when both partners can make an effort to have sex makes it a priority.

Maybe sometimes it happens and other times not, but it keeps nurturing the sex life, putting it in the forefront of the relationship.

Good Communication Regarding Sexual Needs

As couples become familiar with one another there is danger of taking each other for granted, especially in a sexual relationship. Make sure this doesn't happen. Keep the level of interest high and the experience mutually fulfilling. To do this, you need to engage in one of the chief ingredients for having a great sex life: good communication. The best sexual partners practice unselfish love. They want to know exactly what their partner needs to feel the most deeply loved and sexually satisfied. They explore what their mutual needs and wants are, probing to get specifics in how to touch one another, what to say and do, how they'd like their partner to dress, etc. This kind of exploration also needs to happen regarding what partners need to best prepare them to get in the mood. This is especially important for women. What women need emotionally in order to feel receptive sexually is important. There can be big differences between partners regarding sexual desire, which also needs to be discussed openly and respectfully to arrive at mutually agreeable compromise.

Self-Exploration Exercises

Explore each of the four areas of relationship closeness with your partner:

1) *Conversational Intimacy*
Examine the amount of time that you spend talking together and look at what gets in the way of taking more time. What do you talk about? Are there conversational areas that you can expand beyond the usual, *How was your day?*

2) *Shared Interests and Activities*
Are there ways that you can develop more shared interests and activities together? Take time to brainstorm new interests and things to do together.

3) *Physical Affection*
In what ways can you be more affectionate with one another? And what are the specific ways each of you desires affection? Do these relate to love needs?

4) *Sex*
Are you taking enough time for your sexual relationship? Have you openly and honestly shared what you like and dislike? Are there other ways to enhance your sexual intimacy further?

Next, we will go beyond the four types of closeness to other skills for building and energizing positive feelings of love, passion, and romance for taking your relationship to the very highest level possible!

The Relationship Co-Coaching Model for Dynamic Growth

1. Fulfill Partner's Love Needs
2. Identify and Change Negative Relationship Patterns (NRPs)
3. Reduce Conflict with Softly Specific Co-Coaching
4. Seek Relationship Self-Actualization and Altruistic Love

Chapter 11

Positives, Love Affirmations, and Romantic Flirting

So don't waste any time! Go back to your partner and surprise her or him with your renewed romantic efforts—revitalize the love and passion in your relationship.

I hear from couples all the time who say, *I know we should be more loving and more romantic with one another, however we just don't have the time or energy*. And they ask me what they can do to create a more romantic, passionate relationship.

My response is that there are clearly defined practices to deepen the emotional love bond. *Yes, there are skills to intensify positive feelings of fondness and love.* Sustaining wonderful feelings of love in a relationship won't just happen by itself.

You can decide to proactively say and do those things in a relationship to create positive energy and feelings, or you can sit back and comfortably cruise. The question you have to ask yourself is, *do I want more in my relationship?* If the answer is yes, then consider the possibility that you can consciously create deeper feelings of love.

The first of these intentional love practices are the four principles of our co-coaching model presented in Section One. What a surprise! These are the foundational elements, which at first glance might not appear very passionate or romantic. However, they are the building blocks for sustaining enduring love. Without them, tender feelings of vulnerability, love, and romance can be very difficult to maintain due to non-change beliefs, repeating NRP conflict, and self-centered love. Hence, the same assumption is made here as in the last chapter, that one has addressed any underlying negative feelings from recurring relationship conflict that would interfere with taking the next steps.

Four Best Practices for Sustaining Passion and Romance

To create a really fabulous relationship you'll want to pay attention to the following set of four practices to build in deeper love, positivity, and romance:
1) Positives: Compliments and Appreciation
2) Love Affirmations
3) Loving Acts of Kindness
4) Romantic Flirting

The Power of Positives and the Five-to-One Ratio

First, let's discuss positives which are most commonly expressed in the form of compliments and appreciation. We live in a culture that normally does not promote giving positives to one another. Instead, we tend to focus more upon pointing out those things that are wrong or need correcting, rather than things done well. This tendency occurs in business, traditional parenting, and especially romantic relationships. Most people just simply aren't very skilled at giving recognition and appreciation to others.

We know from the Gottman research that couples in stable, happy marriages have a higher positive-to-negative ratio (5:1) when speaking to one another during conflict. The ratio is only .8 to 1 in couples heading toward divorce. So, it would seem that these happier couples have intuitively grasped the importance of positives.[30]

One thing's for sure: it bodes well for one to give a high frequency of positives to others in all aspects of life. Surveys of employees show that their most powerful motivator was personalized, instant recognition from comments by managers.[31] I think most people would agree that the world would be a better place if everyone were more conscious about giving compliments and appreciation to others.

The scarcity of positives given in both business and marriage seems to be due, again, to underlying societal beliefs. For example, in my executive coaching work I often get pushback from managers when first introducing the idea of inspiring employees by giving a higher frequency of positives. Their first response typically is that they do give compliments, when they're deserved. This generally means that the employee must do an obviously outstanding job in order to be deserving of the positive comment.

Similarly, when counseling with parents and sharing with them alternative methods for motivating children by being more positive, I often hear a similar response. For example, their children typically don't do a good enough job to be complimented on a more regular basis.

In cases of coaching business leaders *and* parents, I explain to them the fundamentals of positive reinforcement: There should be emphasis upon giving more positives for *any and all efforts in the desired direction*. This means any behavior that's directed toward improvement is one that needs to be reinforced.

Positives Enhance Self-Esteem

This simple approach will also prove valuable in one's romantic relationship. Appreciate all progress; your partner doesn't have to be perfect! He or she is likely working hard in life, often frustrated, stressed and at times experiencing insecurities and self-doubts. Giving more compliments and appreciation will serve as a refreshing wave of love that supports positive self-esteem. This will make one's partner feel great. It's an excellent way to show commitment to the goal of self-actualization by thinking unselfishly about a partner's needs. This serves to heighten the emotional love bond, nurturing it further.

You can make a commitment right now to give your partner more positives to help them feel better and solidify deeper love feelings. If you want your partner to feel more romantic feelings for you—and you for them—one of the best ways is to become a continual source of positivity for one another. If each of you becomes the most esteem-enhancing person in the other's life, then isn't this going to naturally deepen your feelings of love for one another?

At the same time, why don't we all practice giving more positives to everyone throughout the day, especially in the workplace and with other family members? It's particularly important to remember this with children, where we can directly build self-confidence.

Wouldn't it be great if in our society everyone paid more attention to practicing the skill of spreading positives among all people encountered during the day? If we practice this with others, it becomes easier to remember with our romantic partner.

In reinforcing positivity with clients, I have a ritual of starting every therapy session by asking them to turn, face one another, and give each other a positive. It can be something regarding efforts made with the homework for that week or anything positive about the other person. This is particularly important since couples often want to immediately jump into heated issues; it helps to begin with a reminder of loving feelings for one another.

Love Affirmations

The next love-deepening practice is the concept of love affirmations. These refer to expressions of deep caring and admiration for one's partner. This is done in a way that fully envelops the other person in feelings of being truly loved. It affirms partners at the core of their being, leaving them with a wonderful feeling. In short, it gives them what every person really wants, namely to feel completely and fully loved!

Now here's the hitch: If you're like most people, this doesn't necessarily come very easily for you. It requires some thought and reflection about how you really do feel about your partner and takes some creativity in selecting the right words. This is something that most people rarely do often enough in their relationship. You probably witnessed very few of these kinds of loving verbalizations modeled by your own parents in their marriage, and societal messaging rarely emphasizes it.

What we're talking about here is the skill of saying things to your partner that helps them feel good, respected, and loved. The picture of romantic love painted in the entertainment industry makes it look like it just happens all by itself very easily, doesn't require many words, and is primarily expressed through sex.

However, to maintain deep love past the stage of infatuation and romance, there does need to be a recharging of deeply positive, emotional feelings, even while going through the daily routine of life. This is a romantic love practice of the self-actualized partner. It's unselfish love at its best. We are consciously attempting to help our partner feel the most deeply loved, secure, and fulfilled that he or she possibly can.

It's very rare in our society for couples who have been together for a while to say such things to one another. Most people are exceedingly unskilled in this way. There may be occasional affirmations in the beginning stages of a romantic relationship, however this usually tapers off as the relationship moves forward and feelings of comfort set in. Life happens, busyness takes over, and cruise control is turned on in a relationship. Add in the frustrations over love needs not being met and the challenge NRP conflict presents—all contribute to keeping a couple from connecting at the deeper emotional level.

Thus, one of the most important gifts you can give your relationship is the love affirmation. It enhances the deep emotional attachment and love for one another even while dealing with all the complexities of life.

Stop and Take Time for Love Affirmations

Let's look at an example of a love affirmation. It's evening, and dinner has just finished. Your children are off to do their homework, take baths, and go to bed. As you're clearing the dinner table, you look at your spouse and feel a warm feeling of joy or affection. Stop what you're doing for a moment and enjoy those feelings further. Think about how nice it is to be in a relationship with your partner and to both have the same desires and be committed to each other. Nurture this moment a while longer; deepen this feeling. Turn to your spouse, take his or her hand in yours saying, "Honey, it's so great being married to you. We have so much in common and I love doing everyday things with you like just now in clearing the dishes. I love you so much."

Now, that's a love affirmation! How often do you stop what you're doing, look into your partner's eyes, and say such deeply felt affirmations? Like most couples, your answer will probably be not often enough.

I've never really had any clients who objected or reacted negatively to the idea of love affirmations. Everyone intuitively grasps its importance. But like anything else, it's a matter of habit and skill. Yes, you're hearing this once again: Becoming the most loving partner you can be requires skill. Sustaining deep love and romance doesn't happen by magic; it occurs because you have two people who set the intention to make it happen. This is indeed the *magic*!

Many people seem to feel almost entitled to a happy marriage, as though all they have to do is passively exist in the relationship and by virtue of this they should have the fantasy of love and happiness. The only problem is that it takes a lot more than this to really sustain a deep, romantic, passionate love over many years.

Love Affirmations Are Romantically Poetic

Love affirmations can go beyond partners' stated love needs, extending into a realm that's almost romantic poetry. Sure, this isn't an easy thing to do at first. And it may take going outside of your own comfort zone. I've found in coaching clients in the basic process of love affirmations that it's really important for them to get over the initial feeling of awkwardness.

Love affirmations are particularly helpful in a couple's therapy session where many negative feelings are being shared, especially during the first few sessions. I often have couples end a session with love affirmations. It helps them reconnect with loving feelings, particularly if they've been discussing heated issues.

One A Day!

In fact, with all couples I give homework of a minimum of one love affirmation a day. Just as with Softly Specific and other skills in this book, it requires practice.

When first experimenting with having couples practice love affirmations, I found they really liked the experience but often found it difficult to find the right words to say to each other. Finally, one couple asked me to give them more examples of the language and wording for what partners might say to one another.

So I went ahead and gave them a whole list, which they really appreciated. Some readers may initially assume that this is artificial. However, the idea here is to expand the repertoire of love language you might use while reflecting the sincere feelings you have towards your partner.

Increase Your Love Vocabulary

Look at it this way: It's just like increasing your vocabulary. Learning new words that can express feelings is valuable. Use the phrases that particularly resonate with you. You may choose to borrow the entire wording, or just phrases that you feel most comfortable with. Everyone really loves to hear their partners say these kinds of things to them. Here's the list:

- I'm so happy that I married you
- You're my best friend
- I've never loved anyone like I love you
- You mean more to me than anyone else
- I love hanging out with you and just being together
- We're a great team; we work so well together in getting things done like cleaning up the kitchen and other things around the house
- I love talking with you
- I love moments like these, sharing things with you even for just a few minutes
- I appreciate that we can talk about anything
- You're the very best partner for me!
- You can feel secure that I'll always be faithful to you
- There's no one out there better for me than you
- I really love the way you look
- I really love [your hair, face, eyes]
- I think you're really pretty, beautiful, or handsome
- I think you're so attractive
- I love that you're very smart
- You're really sexy, hot, etc.

One thing to remember in giving love affirmations is to be really in the moment emotionally. Be physically close, touch each other, and be affectionate. Look into each other's eyes. Let your partner see and feel the depth and intensity of your emotional feelings; touch him or her with great tenderness or passion.

When you sincerely express these things for your partner you'll find that it gives both of you a deep emotional love connection. It's this feeling that helps create passion and romance in a relationship over the long haul.

Stretch Yourself to Affirm Your Partner

Now, maybe you're someone having more significant problems in your relationship. If so, don't be alarmed if you're feeling unable to say any of these things to your partner due to built-up resentment or anger. Once you begin to heal those feelings and change NRPs you'll become more receptive. Stretching yourself to make love affirmations, though, can help facilitate that healing.

Here's a good example of the profound impact that love affirmations can have for a relationship. In the third session with a couple, the wife shared her long-standing feelings that her husband did not express how he cared about her. This was a primary love need for her; specifically she did not feel "important" in his eyes. He had shown extreme difficulty in expressing his feelings. It was very hard for him to find the right words to communicate. I asked him to tell his wife how he really cared about her. The husband, who ordinarily processes things very slowly, took a very long pause for one–two minutes while he thought about it. Then he dispassionately said "There are two things to me that are the most important in life—climate control and you."

Well, needless to say, his wife was not very pleased with this response, even though from his vantage point he was sincerely sharing how important she was to him. Since he obviously lacked the language and words to help her feel loved, I introduced the couple to love affirmations. I gave them the handout with the same examples of love affirmations noted above and asked them to practice sharing deeper feelings for one another during that session. Their follow-up homework was to give one another at least one love affirmation a day, relying on the handout to get a feeling for the type of language to use.

Well, the couple did this homework with a remarkable result! In the following session, they reported a real breakthrough in which the wife said to her husband:

> This week was really good. The love vocabulary makes it so much easier in the relationship. It's the one thing I've been asking for the past 10 years from you, and you hadn't given it. But now you're doing it! That's what I was asking for; that was the biggest deal. It helps me feel like you really love me and you are my partner—I haven't felt that way in many, many years!

Her husband shared happiness about how she was talking to him in a much nicer, less angry way. She commented about the reciprocal effect: *it's been much easier to do so because I'm getting the one thing I need. Instead of the vicious circle* [of frequent arguments], *it's a love circle!*

This is a wonderful illustration of how love affirmations can heal and transform a relationship. However, I'd like to share with you another touching story of how using love affirmations can also have surprising effect on other family members. One couple fully embraced the concept of love affirmations and decided to spontaneously e-mail all of the things they really loved and appreciated about each other. Later, they posted these love affirmations on the kitchen refrigerator as a reminder for one another to see.

Now, it's important to mention they never directly spoke to their children about what they were doing. One week later each of them received an e-mail from their son (age range 10-12) containing a set of love affirmations expressing all the things he deeply loved and appreciated about each parent! This is a beautiful example of the radiating effect of modeling the best practices of love for children.

Loving Acts of Kindness

The next practice for enhancing passion and romance in your relationship is to perform loving acts of kindness. This refers to acts of intentional kindness and unselfishness. These can be things that partners really appreciate or something special they might like. It might be a back rub, helping them out with a household task, asking to get them something from the refrigerator when getting up from the sofa, a foot massage—anything that expresses care.

Of course, there are the time-honored, always welcome traditional forms of expressing romantic feeling—flowers, candy, cards, poetic writing. And in the age of equality these gestures need not be limited to one gender or the other. On the first date with my wife, *I* cooked dinner for her and *she* brought me flowers!

There's also the wonderful practice of leaving little affectionate love notes for one another in a cupboard, briefcase, bathroom mirror, bed pillow, or other places. These are always deeply appreciated. The practice of loving gestures is an actual demonstration of love in a way that's undeniable because it's displayed in outward behavior. Saying the words *I love you* is easy. It's an entirely different thing to go out of your way to show it with actions.

More Supportive Research

There is additional research relevant to the use of positives, acts of kindness, and love affirmations as powerful love practices. Dr. Teri Orbuch, in a large-scale longitudinal study of couples, found a significant difference between happy couples versus unhappy couples regarding "positive affirmations." Three-fourths of the happy couples reported that their spouses often did things to help them feel cared for or special, but less than half of unhappy couples did so. Orbuch says, "Doing or saying small things frequently to make your partner feel special, cared for and loved ... is very predictive of staying together, being happy and [preventing] divorce. These simple actions could be just a loving note in a spouse's wallet or a shoulder rub."[32]

Romantic Flirtation

The fourth practice for love deepening is romantic flirtation. This is most important, of course, for long-term relationships that have moved well beyond the initial stage of infatuation. It's so easy in marriage for passion and romance to diminish. In fact, many married couples I counsel express surprise when I ask them how much they flirt with one another. The idea of marital flirting is foreign to many couples. In fact, their underlying assumption is that because of the daily responsibilities of life, children, and work, this really isn't possible. It's as though flirting is something that's not realistic to expect in a marriage.

However, if one logically thinks about it, this doesn't have to be true at all. It's simply a matter of making it a priority in your relationship.

Let's define what a marital flirtation might look like. Of course, we're only talking about flirtations with your own partner, not with others outside of the marriage. Some might say that innocent flirtations with others outside of the relationship are of no harm. But keeping a strict boundary is extremely important; flirt only with your partner (see the chapter on affairs and how to avoid them).

Examples of Flirtation

To illustrate, examples of marital flirtation would be joking and teasing in an affectionate way. One always has to be careful, of course, when teasing your partner so it does not leave him or her feeling put-down or ridiculed. I tease my wife quite often. However, sometimes the teasing is, in my wife's words, "a bad joke" or borders on something she might perceive as a little too negative.

When she lets me know this, I tell her: *Honey, I'm just acting like the boy on the playground pulling the pigtails of his favorite girl because he likes her so much.* Whenever I say this, any negative feelings on her part immediately leave and she feels affirmed. She'll tell me how much she loves hearing me say this because she knows I'm trying to flirt with her.

The point being made here is that in making efforts to flirt, you may not always be perfect in your delivery. If so, just sincerely apologize and let your partner know your intentions were to try and connect by flirting. In all likelihood, you'll be quickly forgiven.

Another example of flirtation: As you walk by your spouse, you might want to affectionately touch them. My wife and I have a little flirtatious thing we both do with one another. I may be busy doing something in the kitchen and as my wife walks by, she'll lightly bump up against me as though it happened accidentally. It's like a little love bump. We'll both do this at times with one another, just a little way of saying *I'm flirting with you—playing with you,* without having to say it in words.

Many opportunities arise in the daily routine of life. Bring romantic flirtation into your relationship. While you're cleaning the kitchen or taking the kids to an activity, take time to flirt with your partner. Another way of connecting in a relationship that overlaps with flirtation is being playful and silly. With all the seriousness and difficulties in life, it gives joy and reduces stress.

And flirtation can be vital to maintaining a relationship. Research by Dr. Brandi Frisby suggests that flirtation may be helpful in differentiating which marriages will persevere. She found partners who flirted with each other tended to be more satisfied and committed.[33]

These Love Practices Are Synergistic

Actually, all four of these practices for deepening romantic love overlap and can be seen as flirtations. Giving partners compliments about the way they look, expressing deeply felt positive feelings for them, all could be viewed as forms of romantic flirtation. Unfortunately, many couples fail to keep romance and passion alive since there are many day-to-day challenges that interfere with our expressions of love. Make the special effort to use love-deepening practices to recharge your marriage.

It's these little things that put a spark in the relationship. You're the most important person in your partner's life. Your romantic love bond needs sustenance and one of the best ways to do this is by demonstrable behavior in positive words, love affirmations, loving gestures, and romantic flirtations.

So don't waste any time! Go back to your partner and surprise her or him with your renewed romantic efforts—revitalize the love and passion in your relationship. And keep doing so for all of your days together!

Self-Exploration Exercises

Think about how well you practice each of these four ways of enhancing your relationship through positive energy, romance, and a deeper love connection. Explore these areas with your partner and decide where you want to make improvements. Then help each other stay focused on maintaining these romance-sustaining behaviors.

1. Positives, Compliments, and Appreciation
2. Love Affirmations
3. Loving Gestures
4. Romantic Flirting

The Relationship Co-Coaching Model for Dynamic Growth

1. Fulfill Partner's Love Needs
2. Identify and Change Negative Relationship Patterns (NRPs)
3. Reduce Conflict with Softly Specific Co-Coaching
4. Seek Relationship Self-Actualization and Altruistic Love

Chapter 12

Co-Create The Deepest, Most Long-Lasting Love!

Achieving deep abiding love and relationship self-actualization is a noble goal, truly a great life achievement.

Okay, now you're ready to go it on your own. Working to create a consistently deep love and satisfaction in your relationship over many years is an exceptional achievement. Of course it requires the continuous attention of unselfishly meeting love needs and nurturing positive energy in the relationship. It's expected that both of you will experience hurts or slights in the busyness and stress of daily living. This is perfectly natural and normal. But now you can be much better prepared to handle these feelings more effectively through co-coaching.

All of this may seem like a lot of information to digest. Take your time, invite your partner to read this book and explore the beliefs that form the foundation of your relationship. Try to determine how limiting societal beliefs may have influenced you both. Spend time together in identifying your NRPs and the unique ways each of you need to feel deeply loved. Co-coach each other using Softly Specific. Explore how you might make relationship self-actualization the highest priority in your lives, and how you can better express altruistic love for one another.

Watch out for the potential barriers. Keep the emotional love bond strong in your relationship by continual nurturing: giving each other love affirmations, positives, love gestures, and romantic flirtations.

Seek a Professional—Learn the Skills

If you have significant relationship problems, however, don't make the mistake of trying to solve them on your own. It's not a sign of weakness to get outside expert help. And remember, you don't need to have severe problems where you feel as though you've grown apart, fallen out of love, or are on a constant battleground of conflict in order to get help.

Be proactive to improve your relationship. Make it the best that it can be. Take action if you find any significant unhappiness in your relationship, increased arguing or bickering, emotional distance, or desire for a deeper-felt emotional love. Don't wait the six years, which, as we discussed earlier, is the average length of time most couples take before calling a couples therapist.

Relationship self-actualization does require developing new skills. But it can have immense impact on the quality of your life and what you achieve, beyond just occupational and financial success. Love is more than just the self-centered pursuit of receiving pleasure from another person. Expressing altruistic love takes a very conscious effort on a daily basis.

A Story of Encouragement

Let me share a conversation I had with a client couple. They had been married for over eighteen years. When they first came in both complained of serious relationship problems that had kicked in very soon after the birth of their first child fourteen years ago. Chronic emotional estrangement and lack of communication contributed to deep unhappiness for both of them.

There were reality-based stresses inherent in their relationship: She had a demanding high-level job requiring her to work eighty hours a week. They had lost much of their ability to communicate because both felt deep hurt and resentment. In the very first session, the wife said she had told her husband, "Either we go to counseling or let's just live separate lives."

At the twentieth session, after putting in a great deal of work applying each one of the principles in this book, the couple had completely changed the nature of the relationship. They now have taken control of their NRPs and use the Softly Specific process. Conflicts have been greatly reduced and are rarely present now. I recently asked them to honestly review where they were at in the progress made in their relationship. The highly analytical husband, who started marital therapy being quite skeptical, replied:

She's meeting my needs past the point I expected. The relationship feels happy in the same way it was in the first few years of our marriage!

And when I asked her about her assessment of progress she said:

I feel as happy as I was when we first began dating!

In closing out one of their recent sessions with a love affirmation, the wife took both of her husband's hands, looked in his eyes and in the most sincere, heartfelt way said, "I'm really glad you're my husband!" He responded with a similar affirmation, "I'm so glad you're my wife!"

Achieve Your Highest Level of Relationship Happiness

Think back to those first few months in your relationship and how wonderful they were. Know that it is possible to have those same feelings of deep love no matter how many years have passed. Is there anything that's worth working for more than love? The first and last word in life is *love*.

In closing, I hope that this book has given you new ideas for how to take your relationship to an entirely different level. Achieving deep abiding love and relationship self-actualization is a noble goal, truly a great life achievement. Set your intention, be diligent, and never give up in your efforts to keep your relationship exceptional and passionate. Be ever striving in your efforts to make a truly fabulous relationship!

For more information on Dr. Tim McCarthy and Relationship Co–Coaching visit:
http://www.relationshipcocoaching.com

Private Intensive Sessions:
Couples traveling from any distance may schedule a one or two-day working session with Dr. McCarthy.

Appendix A
Additional Details Regarding Research Studies

2011 Study of Children's Values of Characters in TV Shows

A 2011 study by UCLA psychologist Dr. Patricia Greenfield and doctoral student Yalda Uhls, assessing the values of characters in popular television shows in each decade from 1967 to 2007, was reported in *Science Daily*. During this last ten-year span, fame, (public estimation) jumped from the fifteenth spot to the first spot in 2007, making it the most important value; at the same time being kind to others (benevolence) fell from the second to thirteenth. In 1997, the top five values were community feeling, benevolence (being kind and helping others), image, tradition, and self-acceptance. In 2007, community feeling also fell to eleventh while financial success went from number twelve in 1967 and 1997 to number five in 2007. The two least emphasized values in 2007 were spiritualism (sixteenth) and tradition (fifteenth); tradition had been ranked fourth in 1997.[34]

Self-Actualization and Altruism In Business

In the book *Firms of Endearment* by Raj Sisodia, Jag Sheth, and David Wolfe, the authors selected thirty companies they identified as "firms of endearment," companies emphasizing humanistic qualities. Using an extensive selection process, the authors identified thirty companies they believed best exemplified a high standard of humanistic performance in how they treated all stakeholders. (Importantly, they did not use financial performance as the primary criterion for initially selecting the companies.) Some of these well-known firms included Southwest Airlines, Whole Foods, IKEA, Costco, Amazon, and Google.

The authors then went about comparing the financial performance of these companies not to just any other average company; instead, they compared them to the eleven companies identified in Jim Collins' bestselling book, *Good to Great*, companies described as going from good to great based on having delivered superior financial returns to investors over a long period of time. Specifically, each of those companies had generated cumulative returns at least three times greater than the market over a fifteen-year period.

In comparing the thirty humanistic firms of endearment to the latter eleven good-to-great companies, the thirty outperformed the eleven by 331 percent. This is a finding of major importance since it demonstrates that self-actualization; unselfish love and caring for others also help companies become more profitable.

Here's a further important comment from *Firms of Endearment*:

> What is a firm of endearment? The title of this book testifies to deep-seated changes in how people see things in mainstream business culture. Consider the words affection, love, joy, authenticity, in pity, compassion, soulfulness, and other terms of endearment. Until recently, such words had no place in business. However, that is changing. Today, a growing number of companies—including every FoE (Firm of Endearment) cited in this book—comfortably embrace such terms. That is why we coined the phrase "firms of endearment." Quite simply a FoE is a company that endears itself to stakeholders by bringing the interests of all stakeholder groups into strategic alignment. No stakeholder group benefits at the expense of any other stakeholder group, and each prospers as the others do. These companies meet the tangible and intangible needs of the stakeholders in ways that delight them and engender affection for and loyalty to the company.[35]

Appendix B
For The Marriage Therapist

Evidence-Based Research and Common Principles of Success:
A 2012 meta-review in the *Journal of Marital and Family Therapy* examined the research on couples therapy outcome over the decade of 2000-2009; two of the five authors of this study are cited elsewhere in this book—Susan Johnson for Emotionally Focused Therapy (EFT), and Andrew Christensen for Integrative Behavioral Couple Therapy (IBCT). This review expressed excitement about the preliminary development of evidence-based common principles found across successful couples treatments that transcend approach. Five principles proposed by Christenson were offered as a "launching point" for more extensive development of universal processes.[36]

Although this effort to define common elements to successful couples therapy outcome is still just in the formative stage, it is relevant to look at how Relationship Co-Coaching therapy reflects Christensen's five principles. Each principle is italicized below with how this approach is congruent with each one respectively:

(1.) *Dyadic conceptualization challenging the individual orientation view that partners tend to manifest.*

This approach places great emphasis on couples challenging culturally transmitted individualistic, self–centered beliefs about relationships. It commits partners to the intentional goal of achieving a self–actualized relationship by making it the highest priority to mutually meet each other's love needs through unselfish love.

(2.) *Modifying emotion–driven maladaptive behavior by finding constructive ways to deal with emotions.*

This therapy is directly aimed at taking control of negative relationship behavior patterns as well as the tendency to express feelings in a verbally aggressive way with generalizations. The Softly Specific Co–Coaching method calls for couples to learn how to share the "softer" vulnerable feelings beneath anger to more effectively communicate and resolve conflict.

(3.) *Eliciting avoided, emotion–based, private behavior so that this behavior becomes public to the partners, making them aware of each other's internal experience.*

The whole purpose of Relationship Co–Coaching is to help couples learn how to more authentically communicate and bring to the surface deeper feelings that have been avoided or are hard to express, and to achieve new awareness/understanding.

(4.) *Fostering productive communication, attending to both problems in speaking and listening.*

The six steps of the Softly Specific Co–Coaching method are designed precisely to foster productive communication. The first three steps focus on how a partner speaks to the other when sharing feelings and delivering feedback. The second three steps are for how the partner listens in receiving feedback, clarifies it, shows empathy, and takes ownership.

(5.) *Emphasizing strengths and positive behaviors.*

This approach places great importance upon positive "love deepening skills" (Section 3 of book) for couples learning how to consciously express more positive behaviors of compliments, appreciation, and flirtation.

All of the above suggests Relationship Co-Coaching therapy is in clear alignment with these five common principles for successful couples outcome.

Cognitive Reframing of Client Resistance

This approach directly challenges client's non-change self-sabotaging assumptions at the beginning of therapy and throughout the process. For readers who are therapists, what's being recommended is the need for cognitive therapy at the very onset in working with couples to help change their deeply conditioned, long-held, non-growth beliefs about love, relationships, and marriage. Regardless of the type of therapy used, challenging these client assumptions will help overcome their resistance to change and optimize therapeutic outcomes. Subsequently, this book is also meant to help support therapists of all theoretical orientations in reframing these client beliefs.

The Marriage Therapist as Coach

Using this kind of direct psychotherapy-coaching approach, couples come to see the logic of why regular practice is needed with Softly Specific, since they see how the pain of their conflict could have easily been avoided. This motivates them to become more diligent. However, there's always a beginning period where clients fail to practice more regularly at home until they see how important it is.

As a therapist I've had a major shift in the way that I practice marriage counseling. It's evident to me that aggressiveness in voice tone and words and generalized negative value judgments are absolutely essential to inciting and maintaining conflict. Subsequently, I've found it a waste of time to reinforce or enable couples that continue to communicate in this way. The more focused I've become in coaching clients in this technique, the more quickly they're able to reform their negative communication patterns and reduce the frequency of conflict in their relationship.

In this approach the therapist actively challenges non-change beliefs, reinforces altruistic beliefs, and coaches clients in the skills of Softly Specific. It entails training clients how to communicate in therapy sessions while emphasizing that the issue is not who's right or wrong; rather, it's the way they go about communicating and trying to solve their problems. They learn to be more respectful in communicating feelings: how to show empathy, take ownership, and genuinely apologize. These are fundamental skills for solving conflict in relationships.

Accountability is shifted to the clients to learn these skills and become more effective in the way they solve whatever issues arise. They're told that there will be many difficult, thorny issues in the future, so they have to learn how to talk to one another in those situations that will, without a doubt, occur. Using this rationale with clients, I've found that over time they begin to take greater responsibility for their own way of speaking to one another in resolving conflicts. And they are able to often dramatically reduce conflict.

While therapists serve as a highly engaged coach, they still use the best of their psychotherapeutic skills to help clients identify and heal deeper vulnerable emotions. Training partners in how to use Softly Specific when sharing these feelings with one another helps set up a protective emotional climate of safety since aggressive voice tone and words and generalizations are prohibited. These two disruptive behaviors ordinarily prevent couples from ever achieving true emotional healing of deeper vulnerable feelings. Thus, Softly Specific is both a psychotherapy method to help speed the healing of deeper emotions and a coaching process to create behavioral change in conflict.

Therapists interested in learning more: visit
www. relationshipco-coaching.com

Appendix C
Healing From Affairs

The approach I use after an affair is to immediately address the couples' opposing needs. Hurting partners are given permission to fully process all the feelings associated with the affair and their unfaithful partners are confronted in the following ways: First, they must take total responsibility for having the affair; they have caused deep hurt and the wound is hard to heal. Core trust and the foundational security of the relationship have been violated so it's their responsibility to step up and be there for the other partner whenever feelings of hurt or insecurity might resurface—no matter how long it takes.

The partner who has violated the trust should be prepared to offer genuine empathy and continued remorse. This isn't a case where once or twice you say *I'm sorry for having an affair*. Rather, the incredible pain and insecurity requires continued understanding, often for a long time. Yet at the same time the betrayed partner needs to begin to move beyond the hurt and resentment in a balanced way, not repressing feelings but not continuously promoting them either. Certainly questions need to be answered and insight needs to be gained about the *why* of the affair, but there does need to be a sincere effort to heal and move beyond the feelings of hurt.

Exploring Pre-Affair Marital Dissatisfaction

Exploring what led to the affair can often prove valuable while during this process, the therapist's position continues to be reiterated in support of the violated partner:

> There's never any excuse for an affair. If you had an affair and were unhappy in your marriage, it was your responsibility

to assert your needs in a stronger way and to push harder for marriage counseling.

Nevertheless, examining the state of the relationship before the affair regarding unmet love needs and NRPs can also offer both partners a focal point for how to improve the relationship. This sets the stage for discovering how to strengthen the relationship and even make it better than before the affair.

In this way, the betrayed partner is validated while the couple gains insight about the pre-affair marital unhappiness. Here's where the four principles of the Relationship Co-Coaching model can often give new hope to a couple, especially if they can successfully begin to emotionally reconnect in positive ways.

For some partners, though, the healing process after an affair is difficult, especially those with a history of many years of emotional estrangement and severe NRP conflict. It can be an emotional tightrope for those couples trying to repair the relationship; some succeed and others may not. However, many couples go through the healing process develop an even happier relationship than they had before the affair.

Index

Acceptance and Change In Couples Therapy (Jacobson and Christensen), 58, 75
affairs, 112–117
    affairs caused by a lack of strong morals, 113
    boundary violations can lead to, 116
    case example, 114
    chain reaction: hurt, anger, and susceptibility, 115
    hope for recovering from, 117
    marital unhappiness and cultural beliefs can lead to, 113–114
    preventing the affair, 116
    society's beliefs can predispose to, 114
    when an affair happens, 115–116
altruistic love, xiii, 24, 83–97
    altruism research and marriage, 88
    case example, 89–90
    how to love less selfishly, 94
    integrating with spiritual and larger life beliefs, 94–95
    positive culture change—self–actualization and altruism in business, 92–93
    research on decline in values of children, 91
    self–centered love dominates, 84
    softly specific supports self–actualization, 95
    taking responsibility for loving your partner unselfishly, 86
    unselfish love: going out of your way, 88
aggressive personalities, 38
    inclination to take leadership roles, 39
aggressive voice tone, 50
anger, 34, 35, 51
apology without justification, 66–67
arguments and how they start, 54-55
authoritarian leadership, 40-41

beliefs sabotaging romantic relationships, viii
    challenging prevailing beliefs about romantic love and marriage, 3, 8
    exposing destructive societal beliefs, 4
    non-change beliefs, 5-6, 24
    three sabotaging beliefs, 103–109

Chapman, Gary, x
    The Five Love Languages, x

Christensen, Andrew,
    softening with vulnerable feelings, 58
    Integrative Couple Therapy, 75
    five common principles of therapy success, 160

closeness in relationships, 131–138
    assessing your conversational closeness, 134
    be creative in finding opportunity, 137–138
    brainstorm for new interests, 135
    building in the four types of closeness, 131–138
    conversational intimacy, 132–133
    finding time to talk in my marriage, 133–134
    good communication regarding sexual needs, 138
    physical affection, 135–136
    remember—negative emotions can affect sexual desire, 136–137
    sexual, 136
    shared interests and activities, 134
    the four types of, 132
    unresolved conflict and lack of, 132
Collins, Jim, *Good To Great*, 92
communication, xi
    mistaken assumptions, 61
    skills to improve and reduce conflict, 32
communications problems, 16, 32, 46
competing needs, 76
conflict, xi
    break the cycle of NRP Conflict, 46
    caused by NRPs, 38
    caused by unfulfilled love needs, 18
    culture supports sloppy resolution, 50
    ending unstoppable conflict revitalizes love, 78
    high respect based resolution, 52
    how to stop, 46
    reduce with Softly Specific Co-Coaching, 47, 52, 54
    reducing conflict, xi
    two primary factors trigger, 50, 52
Co-Coaching (Softly Specific), 46-81
    development of, 48
    the heart of: authentic communication, 50
core emotional grievances, 60
co–create the deepest, most long-lasting love, 154–156
    case example, 155–156

developmental stages in relationships, 10
divorce, iv
    divorce rate, iv
    divorce —and urgent social crisis, vii
    many couples still interested in reconciliation, 106–107
    research (Doherty, Willoughby, and Peterson) on reconciliation, 106–107
    when is it time to divorce, 107–108
Doherty, William, 4, 106-107
    Discernment Counseling, 107
    research on reconciliation, 106–107

Emotionally Focused Couples Therapy (EFT) by Susan Johnson, 22
    recovery rate, 22
    research on EFT, 22
    softening, 58

Firms Of Endearment (Sisodia, Sheth, and Wofe), 92, 158
The Five Love Languages (Chapman), x
flirtation, romantic, 150–151
    examples of, 151–152
    research shows it helps marriage (Frisby), 152
Frisby, Brandi, 152
fulfill your partner's love needs, ix

generalized negative value judgments, 50, 51
General Social Survey (altruism research), 88
Give And Take: Why Helping Others Drives Our Success (Grant), 92
Good To Great (Colliins), 92
Gottman, John, 36
    study of happy marriages, 57
    study of men sharing power, 36
    study of positive–to–negative ratio (5:1), 142–143
Grant, Adam, *Give And Take: Why Helping Others Drives Our Success*, 92
Gray, John, *Men Are From Mars, Women Are From Venus*, 106
Greenfield, Patricia, study of children's values, 91, 158

harsh verbal discipline for children: study of, 41
healing deep emotional hurts, 79

interpersonal skills, v
interpersonal relationship training, vi

Integrative Couple Therapy (Christensen and Jacobson), 58, 75, 160

Jacobson, Neil, 75
Johnson, Susan
    see also Emotionally Focused Couples Therapy (EFT)
    meta-review of couples therapy, 160

Klein, Stefan, *Survival of the Nicest*, 92

love affirmations, 144–145
    are romantically poetic, 146
    case example, 148–149
    love vocabulary, 147–148
    one a day, 146–147
    stop and take time for, 145–146
    stretch yourself to firm your partner, 148–149
loving acts of kindness, 149–150
    research on (Orbuch), 150
love needs, ix
    deeper meaning of love needs, 21
    examples of, 27
    lack of clarity, 25
    meeting on two levels: emotional and behavioral, 21
    relationship to NRPs and reducing conflict, 24
    unbiased self-discovery of, 26
    why couples fail to meet love needs, 22-25
love deepening skills, xiv, 129–153

marital problems: length of time before couples seek help, 32
marriage, iv
    happy marriage research (Gottman), 57
Men Are From Mars, Women Are From Venus (Gray), 106
men sharing power have happier marriages, 37–38

Negative Relationship Patterns (NRPs), x
    aggressive parenting style reinforces, 41
    aggressive personalities, 39
    and conflict, 11, 32
    anticipating the clash of, 34
    authoritarian leadership, 40-41
    case example, 36
    definition of, 32

encountering is normal and expected, 43
erode love, 42
overlap with unmet love needs, 35
reinforced in business world, 40
sexual feelings affected by, 36, 37
top 20 most common, 34

Orbuch, Teri, 150
   research on positive affirmations, 150

passion: four best practices for sustaining, 142
Petersen, Bruce, research on reconciliation, 106–107
positives: complements and appreciation, 142
   enhancing self–esteem, 143–144
   research on (Gottman), 142–143
   the power of positives and the five–two–one ratio, 142–143
positive culture change—self–actualization and altruism in business, 92–93

relationship barriers and sabotage, xiii
Relationship Co–Coaching, ii
Relationship Co–Coaching for Dynamic Growth: Four Key Principles, ix-xiii
   Principle #1: Fulfill Partner's Love Needs
   Principle #2: Identify and Change Negative Relationship Patterns (NRPs), 32-33
   Principle #3: Reduce Conflict with Softly Specific Co-Coaching, 47
   Principle #4: Seek Relationship Self–Actualization and Altruistic Love, 85–86
relationship problems, 6
   caused by failure to fulfill love needs, 16
relationship self–actualization, xiii, 24, 83-97
relationship self–exploration, xiv
romantic relationships—no skills training, vi

Science Daily, study of children's values, 91, 158,
Sisodia, Rag, *Firms Of Endearment*, 92, 158
Sheth, Jag Sisodia, Rag, *Firms Of Endearment*, 92, 158
Smith, Tom (altruism research), 88
societal education, 7
Softly Specific Co–Coaching, xi, 46-81
   acceptance of your partner's flaws, 75
   acceptance of your partner's flaws, 75
   apology without justification, 66–67

assumptions of negative intent, 71–72
backsliding—it happens to the best, 80
being powerfully assertive, 55
case example, 56
case example, 69–70
cautionary note, 49
clarify feedback, 66
development of, 48
downshifting to vulnerable feelings, 58
empathy, 66
feedback for slipped–ups, 72
feedback regarding aggressive voice tone and words, 73–74
feedback regarding generalized criticisms, 74–75
feedback regarding generalized criticisms, 74–75
healing core emotional grievances, 60
it's like an app—a software platform, 79
long–term relationship protection, 80
natural softening agent, 58
objectively defining specific behavior, 60
ownership and apology, 66–67
practice makes perfect, 77
receive co–coaching feedback: stop repeating conflict, 66–81
requires repeated practice, 49
six steps of, 53-54
the heart of: authentic communication, 50
the no–excuses agreement for any verbal aggression, 68–69
three steps for receiving feedback, 65
upshifting from hurt to anger, 60
violations of softly specific, 72–73
stress, managing in relationships, 120–125
  develop self–control regarding emotional grievances, 122
  fun and enjoyment reduce stress, 124–125
  rebelling against perfectionistic society, 123
  reduce stress by expecting imperfections, 121
  stress created by overextension, 122–123
  stress most often is mental, 121
  study shows women still do two–thirds of housework, 125
  too many outside activities, 123–124
Survival of the Nicest (Klein), 92

Uhls, Yalda, study of children's values, 91, 158
University of West Virginia Medical Center, vi

Willoughby, Brian, research on reconciliation, 106–107
Wolfe, David, *Firms Of Endearment*, 92, 158

Notes

1 http://www.apa.org/topics/divorce/, 10-22-14
2 Gary Chapman, *The Five Love Languages: The Secret to Love That Lasts*, (Chicago: Northfield Publishing, 2010),15.
3 William J. Doherty, PhD, *Take Back Your Marriage: Sticking Together in a World That Pulls Us Apart*, (New York: The Guilford Press, 2001), 14-37.
4 Ibid., 94-100.
5 David Olson, *Relational Wellness: Corporate America's Business*, Life innovations Inc., 2012, 7. https://www.prepare-enrich.com/pe/pdf/research/Corporate_America_Business.pdf
6 Press release, *Employees more distracted by their spouse then their cell phone while at work*, CompPsych Corporation, June 12, 2012 http://www.comppsych.com/press-releases-2012/587-June-12-2012,
7 Susan M. Johnson, *The Practice of Emotionally Focused Couple Therapy: Creating Connection*, 2nd ed. (New York: Taylor & Francis Group, 2004), 6.
8 Gottman.com, *Q&A,* Nov. 2011.
9 John M. Gottman, PhD, and Nan Silver, *The Seven Principles for Making Marriage Work*, (New York: Three Rivers Press, 1999),100.
10 "The View From The Top, And Bottom," *The Economist*, (New York: September 24, 2011, taken from the print edition), www.economist.com/node/21530171
11 Ming-Te Wang, Sarah Kenny. "Longitudinal Links Between Fathers' and Mothers' Harsh Verbal Discipline and Adolescents' Conduct Problems and Depressive Symptoms." *Child Development*, 2013; DOI: 10.1111/cdev.12143
12 Gottman and Silver, *The Seven Principles for Making Marriage Work*, 27.
13 John M.Gottman, PhD, *The Marriage Clinic: A Scientifically Based Marital Therapy*, (New York: W. W. Norton & Company, Inc., 1999), 85
14 Gottman and Silver, *The Seven Principles for Making Marriage Work*, 27-34.
15 Gottman, *The Marriage Clinic: A Scientifically Based Marital Therapy*, 226.
16 Neil Jacobson, and Andrew Christensen, *Acceptance and Change in Couple Therapy: A Therapist's Guide to Transforming Relationships*, (New York, W.W. Norton & Company, 1996), 104-10.
17 Johnson, *The Practice of Emotionally Focused Couple Therapy, 184-186.*

[18] Jacobson, and Christensen, *Acceptance and Change in Couple Therapy: A Therapist's Guide to Transforming Relationships*, 20.

[19] Tom W. Smith, "Loving and Caring in the United States: Trends and Correlates of Empathy, Altruism, and Related Constructs," *The Science of Compassionate Love: Theory, Research, and Applications*, Ed.'s: Beverly Fehr, Susan Sprecher, and Lynn Underwood, (West Sussex, United Kingdom, Blackwell Publishing, Ltd, 2009), 81-120.

[20] *Love Secrets of Happily Married Couples: Focus More on Your Partner Than Yourself, Study Shows*, by Miranda Hitti, reviewed by Ann Edmundson, M.D., PhD; Web M.D. Health News, February 9, 2006,1.

[21] *Popular TV Shows Teach Children Fame Is Most Important Value, Psychologists Report; Being Kind to Others Fell Dramatically In Importance Over 10 years*, Science Daily, July 12, 2011,1.

[22] Raj Sisodia, Jag Sheth, and David B. Wolfe, *Firms of Endearment: How World-Class Companies Profit from Passion and Purpose*, (Wharton School Publishing, 2007), 31.

[23] Ibid., 13-17.

[24] Adam Grant, *Give And Take: Why Helping Others Drives Our Success*, (Penguin books, 2013), 6-7.

[25] Ibid., 20-21.

[26] John Gray, PhD, *Men Are From Mars, Women Are From Venus: A Classic Guide To Understanding The Opposite Sex*, (Harper Collins Publishers, 2012), 8-9.

[27] William J. Doherty, Brian J. Willoughby, and Bruce Peterson, "Interest in Marital Reconciliation in Among Divorcing Parents," *Family Court Review*, Vol. 49 No. 2, April 2011, Association of Family and Conciliation Courts, 313-321.

[28] Elizabeth Bernstein, "When It's Just Another Fight, And When It's Over", *The Wall Street Journal*, Tuesday, April 3, 2012, D1–C2.

[29] Pearson, Catherine, *More Men In 'Women's Jobs' Means More Men Chipping In At Home, Study Says*, huffingtonpost.com, 08/13/2013

[30] Gottman, *The Marriage Clinic: A Scientifically Based Marital Therapy*, 35.

[31] Bob Nelson, *1001 Ways to Reward Employees*, (New York: Workman Publishing, 1994), 1.

[32] Anna Miller, "Can This Marriage Be Saved," *Monitor on Psychology*, April 2013, 46.

[33] Frisby, Brandi N., Booth-Butterfield, Melanie, "The 'How' and 'Why' of Flirtatious Communication Between Marital Partners," *Communication Quarterly* (2012), 60 (4), 465.

[34] *Popular TV Shows Teach Children Fame Is Most Important Value, Psychologists Report; Being Kind to Others Fell Dramatically In Importance Over 10 years*, Science Daily, July 12, 2011,1.

[35] Sisodia, Sheth, and Wolfe *Firms of Endearment: How World–Class Companies Profit from Passion and Purpose*, 6.

[36] Jay L. Lebow, Andrew Christensen, Susan M Johnson, "Research On The Treatment Of Couple Distress," *Journal of Marital and Family Therapy*, Vol. 38, January 2012, No. 1, 147.

CPSIA information can be obtained
at www.ICGtesting.com
Printed in the USA
FSOW02n0913070417
32735FS